2006

STREET SMARTS
20 Proverbs for Modern Businesspeople

HAL GOOCH
with Doug Wead

STREET SMARTS
20 Proverbs for Modern Businesspeople

HAL GOOCH
with Doug Wead

Introduction..1		
Proverb 1	If You Snooze, You Lose......................................7	
Proverb 2	Find Your "Why?" and You'll Get Your "How?"...................14	
Proverb 3	Few Things in Life Are Fair.................................21	
Proverb 4	Your First Job Is Yourself"...................................29	
Proverb 5	A Good Plan Is Better Than a Good Man....................38	
Proverb 6	Bend or Break..48	
Proverb 7	Check and Re-check..58	
Proverb 8	You Can't Get Far on Empty................................66	
Proverb 9	A Lone Wolf Eventually Starves..........................75	
Proverb 10	Be a Wise Old Owl…Listen Your Way to Success..................84	
Proverb 11	What Gets Rewarded Gets Done.........................96	
Proverb 12	Trust Is the Coin of the Realm...........................104	
Proverb 13	Don't Talk the Talk Without Walking the Walk.....................111	
Proverb 14	Take Care of the Little Guy and He Will Take Care of You...120	
Proverb 15	Culture Keeps What Enthusiasm Gets................130	
Proverb 16	Be Willing to Learn from the Out-of-Town Expert with the Briefcase..................................140	
Proverb 17	Bloom Where You're Planted.............................151	
Proverb 18	Don't Re-invent the Wheel.................................160	
Proverb 19	Keep Your Eyes on the Clock............................169	
Proverb 20	Persistence Pays..178	
A Final Word..186		

Introduction

"The three great essentials to achieve anything worthwhile are, first, hard work; second, stick-to-iveness; third, common sense."
Thomas Alva Edison

QUESTIONS

For the past 30 years I have been counseling independent businesspeople and while the challenges have varied, the basic questions have never changed.

"How can I improve?"

"How can I make my life better for myself and my family?"

"Why do I face so many challenges?"

"What can I do to take better advantage of my opportunities?"

"Why do I never seem to get ahead?"

My wife Susan and I have asked many of the same questions during our young business life. Thankfully, along the way, we've been blessed to have mentors and teachers who have been able to give suggestions and sometimes provide the answers to many of these crucial questions. We, in turn, have gratefully passed along what we've learned from them.

SOLUTIONS

One of the most important and disappointing lessons we've learned is that while some business people and organizations respond to specific challenges and grow beyond them, most utterly fail, falling from a thousand cuts or simply losing their way in a fog of despair. The companies themselves sometimes still exist on paper, like rusting cars in a junkyard. But the dream has faded and the fire has gone out.

I have never ceased to be amazed at the widespread stress, burnout, bad health, lack of mission, inefficiency, indecision, lack of understanding and stagnation—mostly due to a lack of strong basic foundations. People have often learned things incorrectly, and even in those rare instances when they discover that elusive fact, they are seldom willing to change.

And yet, people CAN learn. People CAN change. I firmly believe that people WANT to do better, get better and live better. That's why we make New Year's resolutions. That's why we read books, attend seminars and listen to cassette tapes. That's why we spend time dreaming about how things should be. That's why we keep "to-do lists." That's why we make commitments and remain hopeful for the future.

Our problem is that we often don't know how to sustain a high level of success, happiness and health.

WHY?

There are many answers, of course, since this is a complex question. The MAIN answer, however, is very, very simple: People don't really understand the process of day-to-day accomplishment. The reason for this lack of understanding is also relatively simple: We have been sold a bill of goods, and we now believe that we can get results without putting forth effort.

After all, we live in a day of digital internet, instant potatoes, fast-food restaurants, ready-to-serve microwave meals, quick-stop convenience stores and zillions of television channels we can watch at the touch of a button. We even have dial-a-prayer if we need momentary inspiration.

As a result, we have been led to think that we can gain knowledge without studying. Or that we can obtain fitness by purchasing a membership in a health club. That we can raise a well-balanced family without prudent parenting, that we can experience real life by popping in a video tape, that we can develop top-flight organizations through well-articulated mission statements and that we can build successful businesses with slick advertising campaigns.

We are not a society of day-to-day accomplishment -- not by a long shot. But let me emphasize again that this attitude doesn't exist because people don't have talents and innate abilities. Our problem is that we seem to have lost our way in the "hands-on how-to's" of achievement. We could be performing at such a high level every day, but we aren't!

CHANGES

After thousands of hours spent with men and women, I have been able to observe, listen, study and track how people feel about themselves and how their concept of self compares with what they really do. In many cases, the people I've tracked have been bright, personable and very talented. They say many of the right words, but most simply don't follow their words with action. Over and over, as I have seen people and organizations fall short, in terms of performance, I have felt compelled to ask WHY? How can they be sitting on top of a great project, a great concept and know what to do but not get it done?

The fact is, based on my experience in working with people from all backgrounds, that anyone can break past barriers and become successful. I know with certainty that fulfillment is not the exclusive domain of a gifted few, but is a process of self-development which can be used by many to bring forth the best from themselves and others. But to do this, the person must learn to manage every area of life on a **day-to-day** basis. Success, as is often-quoted, is hard by the yard but a cinch by the inch!

This book started out as a memorandum to a few selected friends to help them begin to build greater success on a daily basis. Over the years I had developed a comprehensive set of forward-thinking strategies. They certainly weren't original with me, but had been gleaned from the best minds I had been blessed to learn from. I had shared them with business people, clients and business organizations in ballrooms and coliseums across the country but I had never systemized them and put them all together in any chronological order. I decided to call these basic truths STREET SMARTS. They are simple PROVERBS for everyday people who want to do extraordinary things in life. In this extended memorandum, which has now become a book, I have taken the best of those strategies and now present them to you.

Where will you be five years from today—personally and professionally? How about ten years from today? If you want more out of life, and if you desire to create new opportunities for yourself, your family and business associates, STREET SMARTS will help you make a significant difference in your pursuit of success. Enjoy!

--Hal Gooch

Proverb 1
"If you snooze, you lose."

"Now I've burned the last bridge behind me. All through the storm and darkest night, my instincts were anchored to the continent of North America, as though an invisible cord still tied me to its coasts. In an emergency--if the ice-filled clouds had merged, if oil pressure had begun to drop, if a cylinder had started missing--I would have turned back toward America and home. Now, my anchor is in Europe: on a continent I've never seen... Now, I'll never think of turning back."*

--Charles A. Lindbergh

*Quotes and details from Capt. Bob Dawson and Darryl Hicks, *Born to Fly* (Stillwater, OK: New Forums Press, 1990), p. 124. Used by permission of the authors.

OPPORTUNITIES

Unless you live in some very remote part of the world, with nobody around and no resources to speak of, the chances are that sometime in your life a momentous opportunity will appear in front of you. In fact, most people have undoubtedly walked past many wonderful doors of destiny that they completely ignored. It is human nature to become mired in routine and blind to the world around us.

Through personal friendships with hundreds of millionaires in dozens of countries, I have come to this conclusion:

"If you snooze, you lose!"

Here's the life-changing point: To be successful you don't have to be the smartest, the fastest or the strongest—you simply need to be alert to the opportunities all around you. Timing is often everything!

NO RULES

Success is sometimes hard to define. Beyond that, the road to lofty heights of success are often confusing and even overwhelming. The rules of acquiring personal wealth, for example, seem to defy any formula, any proven system. I've met successful people who have lousy work habits. Some don't seem to work at all. I've met many who have no education and some who seem downright ignorant. There are high achievers who are extroverts bursting with enthusiasm, yet others equally prosperous who are so shy that they are practically hermits in their mansions without enough courage to drive a car or order a pizza over the telephone. Some of them have crazy political ideas that just seem to defy any common sense. Many are at least slightly eccentric. Almost all are considered "lucky" by their contemporaries. Here's the common thread: The so-called "luck" of the successful people in the world almost always has something to do with **timing**.

After the fact, all of us can spot a good deal. A stock that shot up, a business that succeeded, a job that led to fortune. But we failed to benefit because we acted too slowly or didn't act at all. In some cases we froze with fear. We thought, "If it's such a good idea why is it just sitting there and nobody noticing?"

You don't have to be a genius to be successful, but you do have to be alert. Timing is everything.

INTO THE CLOUDS

At the turn of the millennium, when the world looked back on a thousand years of history, journalists and historians began to name the most important players, the people who shaped our civilization and made the biggest difference. One of the most unlikely names to surface on virtually everyone's list was that of Charles A. Lindbergh, the first man to make a solo, non-stop flight across the Atlantic Ocean.

HAL GOOCH ♦ *STREET SMARTS* ♦ Proverb 1 ♦ 4

As a child, Lindbergh had a fascination with aircraft. One of his earliest childhood memories was that of a six-year-old, running into the front yard, watching a biplane buzzing above his family home. The rest of that afternoon, he lay on the grass looking up into the blue sky, imagining how much fun he would have, floating up there among the clouds. Lazy afternoons on his back in the grass became rituals to the young Lindbergh. Curiously, he never seemed to dream about the dangers, or imagine the sensation of an emergency crash landing or falling from the shy. As Lindbergh later told his biographers, "I was just interested in getting up there in the clouds." By the time he was a teenager, his dream of becoming a "birdman" (as they were called) had come true.

WINDOW OF OPPORTUNITY

The idea of a Trans-Atlantic flight was on the minds of most young pilots in the 1920's, and Charles Lindbergh was no exception. Theoretically, such a flight was technically possible, so the public clamor and anticipation began to build. Long before Lindbergh's plane left the ground on his historic flight, it was common knowledge that the pilot who completed the task would become a household name. The race was on. As Indiana Jones told Shortround, "Fame and glory, kid; fame and glory."

Lindbergh was convinced that the same dreams that had taken him to the clouds would soon take him into the history books, but he knew that it was going to be a struggle. Already the clock was ticking. Several talented, competing teams had already gained the capital and personnel to make the trip. He could only focus on his own plan and hope that the competition would falter.

HAL GOOCH ♦ STREET SMARTS ♦ Proverb 1 ♦ 5

In Saint Louis, Missouri, Lindbergh finally found a willing group of businessmen, the Robertson Aircraft Corporation, who agreed to contribute the $15,000 start up capital. It was all he needed to begin building his plane. A grateful Lindbergh promised to name his plane the *Spirit of St. Louis*. It would become the most famous plane in history.

There was much more to Lindbergh's success than the 33.5-hour flight. It came as a result of years of dreaming, planning, tireless public relations, courting of financiers, attention to engineering detail and dogged persistence. A.J. Edwards, general manager of Mahoney-Ryan Air Lines, builder of *The Spirit of St. Louis*, once said: "That so-called luck of Lindbergh is a popular fancy that is far away from the truth. Lindbergh won out in his flight because he prepared himself for it. He went over every detail of the specifications and the tests. He insisted on many changes. When the plane was completed, no one was allowed to test it but himself. (Sic.) He took 30 days alone to figure his course, and he worked long hours into the night many times."

But there were three factors that could not be figured accurately until the day of the flight, the weather, the competition and his ability to stay awake. Two of the three were beyond his control.

Lindbergh was not the frontrunner in the race across the Atlantic. Another team had more prestigious corporate and public relations backing. But as fate would have it, the frontrunner stumbled. When the big day finally came, the distinctive, silver monoplane was ready. On May 20, 1927, Charles Lindbergh lifted his Ryan NYP off the New York runway to begin his historic attempt at a solo, nonstop flight.

ENDURANCE

The 33.5-hour, 3,610-mile journey over the Atlantic Ocean proved to be formidable. With seasoned stamina honed as an airmail pilot making all night hauls over starry midwestern prairies, Lindbergh gallantly fought sleep through determination and sheer strength of character. He forced his body to stay alert so he could reach his goal. When he arrived in Paris, a reporter described the young pilot's condition: "As he was lifted to the ground, Lindbergh was pale, and with his hair unkempt, he looked completely worn out."

Today, the world still celebrates Lindbergh's incredible 33.5-hour journey and imagines what it must be like to fight off sleep in such a dangerous set of circumstances. By today's standards, what Charles Lindbergh did was really not incredible at all compared to the reward it gained, but when he landed at Le Bourget Field near Paris, Lindbergh flew into the history books and single-handedly convinced millions of people that the airplane had come of age. Many heralded the event as the biggest development in aviation since the Wright brothers' 1903 history-making achievements at Kitty Hawk, North Carolina. More and more people became interested in aviation as a future. Businesspeople were suddenly more willing than ever to invest money in the industry.

Most importantly, more paying passengers than ever stood in line to ride among the clouds.

But Charles Lindbergh was successful not because he was the best pilot or the best fundraiser or the best engineer. He was successful because he saw a window of opportunity and moved quickly to get through it. Yes, the public called him "Lucky Lindy." After all, he could not control the weather and he could not control the competition. But as I mentioned earlier, timing is almost always a major ingredient of the secret to success. When his opportunity came, Charles Lindbergh was ready.

TIMING

You snooze? You lose.

By staying awake, Lindbergh survived his voyage across the Atlantic Ocean. By being supremely alert, he saw the opportunity in the first place. When it came time to achieve his dream, he was able to overcome obstacles during the life-changing flight.

Stop right now and look around. What opportunities are in front of you? Which fateful openings are you overlooking? What powerful chances are you neglecting? Most importantly, what would it mean for you to tap into those life-changing possibilities?

Proverb 2
"Find your `Why?' and you'll get your "How?"'

"*I see only the objective.
The obstacle must give way!*"
Napoleon

BUILDINGS

For over a quarter-century I've been helping men and women build their own businesses. Almost without exception, most people start out with great enthusiasm and excitement. Likewise, almost without exception, most become discouraged when their initial efforts go somewhat unheralded and seem unfruitful. Some survive this stage of foundation and development. Others simply give up before their enterprises have an opportunity to grow into something wonderful.

Why? What keeps some people moving toward their dreams while others stumble and fall? After years and years of asking that question, it isn't really a mystery. The ones who give up generally understand the "HOW?" of business ownership, but they fail because their "WHY?" isn't big enough.

Let me offer a comparison. Most of my life has been spent less than a half-hour from Greensboro, North Carolina. An hour and half down Interstate 85 is Charlotte. Through the years I've watched as these two nice-sized cities have blossomed into mega-metropolitan areas. I've seen construction crews work over many months and even years while building impressive brick, glass and metal office buildings, coliseums and even a few skyscrapers.

Now, I don't pretend to an engineer, but even an onlooker realizes that building those large structures requires much more than welding a few beams together and installing the glass. In fact, the most expensive and least rewarding part of construction happens in the muddy foundation trenches far below the surface. Frankly, the construction must seem painfully slow and unrewarding before the gigantic framework finally begins to move above the ground level and into the air.

No one considers these seemingly slow, below-the-ground, procedures absurd or illogical. Why then do men and women become puzzled and disheartened when businesses require foundation building long before they become flourishing companies?

Here's the point: You have to know what you want—your WHY? (your overriding reason for building your business) long before you go through the HOW? (your steps to starting and developing your enterprise). In fact, unless your WHY? is larger than your HOW? you will probably get discouraged, disoriented and eventually not succeed. It's that crucial.

Let me share a few guidelines in developing a huge WHY?

DREAM BIG

Anybody can dream. If you want something badly enough, no barrier can stop you; no circumstance can get in your way. The only thing that hinders your dream is you.

HAL GOOCH ♦ STREET SMARTS ♦ Proverb 2 ♦ 4

Author, Dr. Robert Schuller says, "Success will be never ending and failure will never be final for those people who have the capacity to dream." Anyone who has succeeded in the past has developed the ability to dream. So can you!

If fact, you ARE your dreams. They define you as an individual. They direct your behavior. They encourage you toward great achievements.

Thomas Edison was one of history's powerful dreamers. He applied for 1,093 patents in his lifetime, the most ever granted one person. Among them were the phonograph, incandescent electric lamp, motion-picture projector and carbon telephone transmitter—all of which have improved life for nearly everyone who has lived on this earth since Edison.

You might be thinking, "Sure, Hal, Edison's dreams could come true, but that kind of dreaming is too unrealistic for me."

That is not true! If you could have seen me thirty years ago, painfully shy and filled with overwhelming feelings of inferiority, you would know what a miracle I am. My WHY? simply got bigger than my HOW? Eventually I learned ways to overcome my weaknesses. You, too, can achieve great things.

CONVENTIONAL WISDOM...SELDOM RIGHT

HAL GOOCH ♦ *STREET SMARTS* ♦ Proverb 2 ♦ 5

The "facts" were pretty obvious for me three decades ago. I was a furniture worker in Thomasville, North Carolina. I looked at my feet when I spoke to one person, so the idea of speaking to a group of businesspeople was outrageous and terrifying. How could I build a worldwide distribution and consulting business? Thankfully, as history has shown, the so called "facts" or "conventional wisdom" is seldom true, and first impressions are not always right.

Every achiever I've ever known about has gone through unbelievable struggles and succeeded by convincing themselves that the facts did not count. On the other hand, I have discovered when dreams aren't big enough, the facts often become gigantic. That is when we find ourselves reacting, rather than creating, and accepting whatever fate casts our way.

We can do so much more. When dreams are big enough, somehow the facts don't hold us back and conventional wisdom doesn't intimidate. You can do anything you want if your dream is BIG enough!

Expand your mental limits. There is a reason why the top 5% of people are making 95% of the income. It comes down to hard work and big dreams. Success is fueled by a person's vision, the WHY?

IMAGINATION

HAL GOOCH ♦ STREET SMARTS ♦ Proverb 2 ♦ 6

With success, the struggle then means less and less. I can only imagine how it feels for those construction workers as they look proudly at a finished skyscraper rising prominently into the clouds. I doubt they remember the endless hours of painstaking foundation work. But they see the results.

For you, making the initial steps in business or life may seem huge and overwhelming, but gradually, as you follow the same guidelines that have led others to success, you can begin to set higher goals, reach greater aspirations and accomplish successes you never previously considered possible. Your personal achievement starts in your mind. The first step is to know exactly what your problem, goal or desire is. If you're not clear about this, then write it down, and rewrite it until the words express precisely what you want to achieve.

A dream can mean many things. I like Webster's definition best: "to imagine as possible." Basically, when I use the word, I refer to expanding your mental limits, then doing something about it. More than ever I believe "If the dream is big enough, the facts don't count and conventional wisdom is irrelevant."

Why?

All personal success begins with imagination--the dream. The first step is to know exactly what that dream is. Every dream will have problems, of course, but every problem can be overcome when the dream gets bigger than the challenge. This is one of the greatest success secrets in the world.

Hold tightly to your dreams. Remember, if the dream is BIG enough, the facts don't count! Find your WHY? and you'll get your HOW?

Proverb 3
"Few things in life are fair."

"*I love the man that can smile in trouble, that can gather strength from distress, and grow brave by reflection.*"

Thomas Paine

EQUALITY

"That's not fair!"

If you are a parent, undoubtedly you've heard that phrase a zillion times. You heard it in the back seat of the family car. The phrase was almost always spat out during squabbles over toys and privileges. You heard it at mealtimes. It was the weapon of choice during times of discipline. And if you thought your children would outgrow the phrase, you know by now that you were sadly mistaken.

"It's just not fair!

It's heard in every other arena of life as well—schools, jobs, marriages, families, politics and even religion. Have you ever wondered why we use that phrase so often? What makes us think that life should be fair? Is this a uniquely American inspiration? "The land of the free and the home of the brave?" What about "life, liberty and the pursuit of happiness?" Doesn't America promise "equal opportunity" for all? Isn't that the dream?

The fact is that there are few things about life that are fair. Perfect conditions for success hardly ever exist. Granted, one of the strongest symbols of the "American way of life" is expressed in the statement: "All people are created equal." But the hard truth is that some people are created **more equal** than others.

Before you can understand how to become successful from where you are right now--your personal starting point--you need to understand these truths:

- **You never start even with others.** Some people are born with good looks, charm, personality and privilege. Others are born in war torn areas of the world or deserted by parents at birth. You have no control over this.
- **You are influenced uniquely by past events.** Two people can be born into the same city, have the same opportunities, and share many of the same experiences. Yet one of them may excel, while the other goes nowhere. Each of us reacts differently to the same events.
- **The past cannot be changed or controlled.** You cannot change what has already happened. However, you can accept and forgive whatever happens, and you can learn to accept experience as a lesson on your road of life.
- **Life, basically, makes no promise of being fair.** You must accept this bittersweet fact before you can make positive steps toward success.

So, what do you do if your situation hasn't been perfect—when life doesn't treat you fairly? Do you use it as a crutch, a barrier or the springboard to a powerful future?

IF ONLY

Practically any list of great achievers spotlights this fact: Success hardly ever can be based on perfect conditions. If anything, success is usually founded on the worst possible situations.

HAL GOOCH ♦ *STREET SMARTS* ♦ Proverb 3 ♦ 4

History certainly teaches us this:

- LEONARDO DA VINCI is known primarily as the painter of the mystery lady "Mona Lisa" and her intriguing smile. Actually, he was the product of a broken home, an illegitimate child who never saw his mother. He was passed around from family member to family member, and eventually lived with his father and sixteen-year-old stepmother. Despite a horribly dysfunctional childhood, he eventually became the leading artist, sculptor, astronomer, aeronautical expert, botanist, engineer, anatomist, author and illustrator of the 15th and 16th centuries.

- HENRY WARD BEECHER, the extraordinary nineteenth century American minister and author, as a boy was reported to be "a poor writer, a miserable speller, with a thick utterance and a bashful reticence which people took for stolid stupidity."

- BOOKER T. WASHINGTON was born a slave, had an early life of extreme poverty and unfair treatment, and yet became one of the most valued educators, authors and inventors in America's history.

- Blind, mute and deaf from infancy, HELEN KELLER struggled beyond her immense barriers to learn how to read, speak and write. Before her death in 1968 at 88 years of age, she became admired around the world for her speeches, writing and life.

- ALBERT EINSTEIN was so slow in learning to talk that his parents thought him abnormal and his teachers called him a "misfit." His classmates avoided him and seldom invited him to play with them. He failed his first college entrance exam, but a year later he tried again. He became one of the world's most famous scientists.

HAL GOOCH ♦ *STREET SMARTS* ♦ Proverb 3 ♦ 5

☐ WALT DISNEY faced disbelief and eventual bankruptcy when he began developing his vision. Today, the memory of the man who gave the world Mickey Mouse, Donald Duck and Disney World stands as a lasting monument to his phrase, "All our dreams can come true, if we have the courage to pursue them."

Each of these people had enough "facts" to allow them to quit. But something kept them going. As mentioned in Proverb 2, the difference between doers and quitters is usually the size of the dream. More specifically, achievers find a way, while failures find excuses. The giant gulf between these two lifestyles is best illustrated by the difference between the "if only" mentality and the "what if" mindset.

What do I mean?

I have found that most people live on "if onlys:"
"If only my parents had been different, I could have…"
"If only I had a college degree, my life would be…"
"If only I had more money, I could …"
"If only we could move to a bigger house, our family would …

You have to break out of the "if only" trap, refusing to blame failure, unhappiness and every other bad situation. Simply stated, you have to stop saying "if only" and start becoming a "what if?" person. Your dream has to get bigger than the less-than-perfect conditions in your life.

WHAT IF?

A "What if?" person is what Dr. Robert Schuller calls a "possibility thinker." This person refuses to let bad circumstances rule his or her life. The "What if?" person learns to develops a positive outlook on life and strives to achieve visions and goals despite challenges. A dreamer learns to keep going when roadblocks arise. A dreamer says "What if?"

"What if I started my own business and built it into a profitable enterprise? How would that change my life and the lives of others around me?"

"What if I set solid financial goals and worked toward them to achieve financial independence for myself and family?"

"What if I stopped thinking about the struggles of the past and concentrated on future successes?"

A "what if" mentality implies that a person will take self-responsibility for the future. It means that one can begin putting plans into action. Dreaming "what if" leaves little room for negative thoughts. It allows a dreamer to open his or her mind to creative solutions—a new product line, a better way to eliminate diseases, a different method of teaching. People who break out of the "if only" mentality drop the word impossible from their vocabulary. They replace it with "what if" because dreams thrive on possibilities.

SOLUTIONS

Once you understand the fact that perfect conditions exist for very few people, you can begin to free yourself from the "If only" barriers. Once you break loose from those ruts, the better equipped you will be to forge your own successful life. Are you ready to get started?

1. **Take total responsibility for what you've been, what you are and what you will become.** Take responsibility NOW! Don't spend your life blaming yourself or others. Blaming doesn't help anybody. You can only be successful and happy when you start taking responsibility for yourself.
2. **Develop your own dreams.** Others, often well-meaning family and friends, sometimes influence you to do what they want—their dreams. Only you know what you are capable of doing. You have to set your own self-expectations if you want to be the best YOU.
3. **Become obsessed with learning.** No matter where you are, you can take night courses at a local community college or nearby university. In today's video, DVD and cassette era, anyone can take advantage of the abundant array of educational and motivational opportunities. Thousands of these tools beckon you to open the doors to your future.
4. **Seek out mentors and colleagues who will help bring out your best in the future.** If you want to be great, professionally and personally, associate yourself with the

finest and best people. Let me see who spend time with, and I can predict who you are becoming. Choose your friends and mentors very carefully.

You can rise above your circumstances. Be true to yourself. Your dreams make the difference!

WHO ARE YOU?

Successful people seem to be able to overcome bad situations better than others. They are somehow able to sort out the most important things in life and concentrate on their own aspirations. They are a cut above when it comes to seeking innovative, creative solutions.

Success is not a passive activity. It is not an undertaking for wimps! Sometimes achieving hurts a lot. It is seldom easy. People often misunderstand your motives. But truly successful people learn to leave the past behind, to live each day to the fullest, and to build toward the future. Success is built on possibilities ("What if?"), not problems ("If only..."). Upon which one will you build your future?

Proverb 4
"Your first job is yourself."

"The unexamined life is not worth living."

SOCRATES (470-399 B.C.)
Greek Philosopher

FACTS

Lawyers always talk about "due diligence." In layman's language, it means "check it out, and check it out good!" I believe that the key to any success is knowledge. Sun Tzu, the legendary Chinese military genius, is famous for saying, "If you know the enemy and you know yourself, you need not fear a hundred battles."

What **facts** do you need to know? Obviously, knowing as much as you can about others is very important. In fact, I will focus on relationships in other proverbs throughout STREET SMARTS. However, the most important information is often inside you. The more you know about **yourself**, the better you can maneuver through the mental minefields on your way to greater success.

YOU

Without sounding like some new age guru, let me ask, "Who are you? The **real** you." Thales of Miletus, the Greek philosopher, once wrote: "The most difficult thing in life is to know yourself."

Today, 2,600 years later, self-disclosure is frightening to most people. We do all kinds of things to cover up, to keep others from knowing who we really are. We get so good at using masks that we even fake ourselves. But true success is based on real knowledge. You must be willing to be honest enough to allow your real self to be unveiled. You must stop hiding behind fear of exposure or fear of rejection. Don't ignore the opportunity to know yourself. This is the first critical step to self-improvement.

Let's start at a very basic, physical level. In a sentence, **you are one remarkable piece of work,** a miracle of engineering.

Your heart beats an average of 75 times a minute, 100,000 times a day, 40 million times a year--nearly 3 billion times in your lifetime. Your heart pumps nearly 3000 gallons a day, nearly 650,000 gallons a year--more than enough to fill 80 gasoline tank trucks.

Your blood travels over 150 million miles every day.

You breathe over 23,000 times each day.

You inhale 438 cubic feet of air during each 24-hour segment.

You eat over 3 pounds of food daily and drink nearly 3 quarts of liquids.

You speak nearly 30,000 words each day.

You move specific muscles 750 times every 24 hours.

You exercise seven million brain cells during each day.

There are at least several trillion hard-working cells inside you, each so small that it takes 250 of them, placed side by side, to equal the size of a small speck.

Your inner ear can detect 15,000 different tones, as well as controlling your equilibrium.

Even though your brain will forget more than 90% of what you learn during your lifetime, it will still store 10 times more information than in the 20 million volumes within the Library of Congress.

"Okay, Hal," you may be thinking, "but what do all these numbers mean in terms of success and achievement as a businessperson? One can only measure success compared to others."

We'll get there, but first start by placing value on your life as God has given it. Even those with the most severe handicaps, were created awesomely to do equally awesome feats in life. Why else would God make you so incredibly complex?

KNOW YOUR VALUES

What you do with your magnificent machine—your body—is based on values, inspired by your mind and spirit. Everyone is guided by values, whether those values are recognized consciously or not. It is crucial to assess and to constantly reassess the values that are being reflected in your actions.

King Solomon once wrote, "Wisdom is the principal thing; therefore get wisdom. And in all your getting, get understanding." (Proverbs 4:7). Before you can understand others, you must learn to understand yourself better.

For starters, what are your values? A value is a cherished idea. Once one's value system is clarified, it provides focus. By contrast, people who seem to have no direction are typically those without a guiding purpose or a coherent set of deep beliefs.

The differences between non-values-based and values-based people are obvious. People without a clarified value system tend to look only at results that can be easily measured--an "A" or "B" grade in school, a college degree, shooting a 72 in golf, a job title, an amount in a bank account. Values-based people, by contrast, seem to express their core beliefs by measuring themselves against themselves, by doing their best. And measuring success in quality terms--educational pursuits, achievement, enjoyment, innovation, personal growth, self-esteem and satisfaction.

One of the most important manifestations of STREET SMARTS is a well-honed ability to clarify your own personal values. Here is a "values inventory list" to get you going.

THE "YOU" INVENTORY

Write a complete sentence for each of the following phrases. Jot down the first thing that pops into your mind.

(1) My greatest priorities in life are:

(2) My best talents, personally and professionally, are:

(3) My life is:

(4) Ten years from now, where will I probably live?

HAL GOOCH ♦ *STREET SMARTS* ♦ **Proverb 4 ♦ 6**

(5)   Ten years from now, what will I be doing?

(6)   Ten years from now, what assets will I own?

(7)   Ten years from now, will I be happy?

(8)   More than anything, I want:

What do your sentences say about your hopes for the future? When you think through your values, you begin to understand what controls your approach toward life. Once you know the values that affect your attitude about excellence and quality, you will discover the principles that are already impacting your future.

Values are absolutely vital to personal excellence. If you don't feel good about yourself, you will reject many of the good things that come to you.

These are all reasons why you have to KNOW YOURSELF. Recognize the fact that you were created for a unique purpose. Develop your own clear set of God-given values, and live by them! When you understand your purpose, you understand yourself. When you understand what makes you tick deep inside, you are more prepared for the success you are becoming.

RESPONSIBILITY AND DESIRE

Go back and re-read your answer to the final question in the "YOU" INVENTORY: "More than anything, I want _____." Whatever you wrote in that blank, let me ask the following question. **Just how much do you want it**?

HAL GOOCH ♦ *STREET SMARTS* ♦ Proverb 4 ♦ 7

Seeking to know yourself—what you truly value and really want--must become an all-consuming, driving mission. It's that important!

What do I mean? Let me answer with a story that has been passed down through the centuries. A young man came to Socrates one day with an urgent request. "I have walked 1,500 miles to gain wisdom and learning," the student began. "I want learning, so I came to you. Can you give it to me?"

Socrates spoke without hesitation: "Come, follow me."

The acclaimed teacher led the student to the seashore. He walked into the gentle waves until he and his young follower were in water up to their waists. Then Socrates grabbed his youthful companion and pushed his head under the water. In spite of the younger man's frantic struggles, the teacher held him under the surface. After several tense moments, Socrates pulled the young man out of the water, laid the would-be pupil on the shore and returned to the marketplace. When the young man regained his strength, he walked back to Socrates.

"You are a man of learning and wisdom," the young man challenged furiously. "Why did you treat me so badly?"

"When you were under the water," Socrates asked, "what was the ONE THING you wanted more than anything else?"

HAL GOOCH ♦ STREET SMARTS ♦ Proverb 4 ♦ 8

"I wanted air!"

Then Socrates said, "When you want wisdom and understanding as badly as you wanted air, you won't have to ask anyone to give it to you. You will get it wherever and whenever you can!"

From years of dreaming and planning with thousands of small business people, Susan and I have come to the conclusion that a definition of success must come from within—deep inside. And the desire to reach it must come from within as well. Both the dream and the desire will spring from our values. The sooner we know them and understand them, the sooner our real journey can begin.

UNDERSTANDING SUCCESS

I've always been impressed with people who overcome overwhelming odds on the road to success. Larry Bird is one of those unique people that I admire. As a player, he won every major distinction professional basketball bestows on its players. He was the MVP in 1984, 1985 and 1986. He was named to the all NBA First Team for nine consecutive seasons from 1980-1988. He was a twelve-time NBA All-Star, including ten times elected by the fans to start, and All-Star Game MVP in 1982. His Celtics won the World Championship in 1981, 1984 and 1986. He was the NBA Playoffs MVP in 1984 and 1986. Larry was a vital part of the 1992 Olympic "Dream Team" that won gold medals for the United States. After retirement as a player, he served as a special assistant

HAL GOOCH ♦ *STREET SMARTS* ♦ Proverb 4 ♦ 9

with the Celtics, then joined the Indiana Pacers and accumulated a new trophy case of honors, including "Coach of the Year," his first year of coaching on any level! In 2000, after announcing his retirement, he led his team to the world championship finals.

Through everything—the successes and failures--Bird's true strength is revealed in his statement that has been quoted many times in television interviews and magazine articles:

> "To me, a winner is someone who recognizes his God-given talents, works his tail off to develop them into skills, and uses those skills to accomplish his goals. Even when I've lost or when the situations haven't been the best, I've learned what my weaknesses were, and I've gone out the next day to turn those weaknesses into strengths."

Before you can answer "What do you want to be?" you must figure out where you are right now? What makes you tick? What do you need to change before you can achieve more in life? How can you, as Larry Bird insists, turn your weaknesses into strengths?

Consider this: Most of us try to change other people to achieve our goals. We do not need to change others; we need to change ourselves. Others change as we change our thoughts about them. You see, having strong values is no accident. Success is no accident. Failure is no accident. Success and failure are the result of your values, your choices, your actions.

Those are the **facts** that matter most!

Proverb 5
"A good plan is better than a good man."

"To accomplish great things, we must not only dream, but act, not only believe, but plan."

ANATOLE FRANCE

BEYOND DREAMS

During World War I, German submarines were causing considerable concern for the Americans. During a gathering, cowboy satirist Will Rogers was asked, "What would you do about the subs if you were president?"

"That's easy," the humorist grinned. "I'd drain the Atlantic Ocean dry, and then you could see all of those machines and could blow `em up."

"How in the world could you drain the ocean dry?" an onlooker inquired incredulously.

"Look," Rogers replied, "I came up with the idea. Now, you smart guys figure out how to get it done."

In his unforgettable manner, Will Rogers described the plight of so many big dreams (and would-be dreamers). Coming up with ideas and standards is the easy part. Putting together an action plan to carry out those dreams is the difficult component.

In Proverb 1 of STREET SMARTS, you read about the importance of timing. In Proverb 2, I talked about the importance of dreaming big enough dreams. In Proverb 3, you hopefully discovered ways to overcome life's tendency to be unfair. In Proverbs 4, you were encouraged to dig deeper inside yourself to discover what your true values are.

Now, in Proverb 5, let's take another logical step—putting your dreams and visions and values into a daily, weekly, monthly and yearly action plan.

Learning to develop your dream into a panoramic vision is hard enough. Drafting and carrying out a plan of action is even more difficult. That is why so few dreams survive.

GOALS

Abraham Lincoln wrote: "If we could first know where we are, and whither we are tending, we could better judge what to do and how to do it."

Once you have a huge WHY? (your vision and dreams), go to work on your HOW? Start developing your HOW? by breaking your dreams into targeted goals. You see, your vision empowers your dreams, and your dreams fuel your goals. Fulfillment of those dreams comes through realistic goal-setting on these three levels:

Aspirations rise and fall on your goals and through your dreams. No plan is ever any better than the goals on which it is founded. Take a look at seven ways to make goals work for you:

HAL GOOCH ♦ *STREET SMARTS* ♦ Proverb 5 ♦ 4

(1) **Your goals must be achievable.** A goal is not some vague "pie-in-the-sky" pipe dream or absurd fantasy. A good goal is one which causes you to stretch all your abilities, but one you're reasonably confident you can reach. Only you know the difference between a dream and a fantasy.

To have meaning, goals must be broken down into three categories:

☐ Long-range goals cover several years, but usually not more than 10.

☐ Intermediate goals are set by breaking long-range goals down into annual, or semi-annual steps, always leading toward the long-range goals you have set.

☐ Short-range goals come from breaking down your intermediate goals into monthly or weekly steps toward your long-range goals.

Defined and pursued dreams and goals give direction to your life. Without these life-directors, you will get discouraged and lack the persistence to keep piercing walls of resistance. The secret of goal setting is to learn how to employ motivation and a system of positive accountability. You must have long-range goals to keep you from being frustrated by short-range failures.

HAL GOOCH ♦ *STREET SMARTS* ♦ Proverb 5 ♦ 5

Everything you do now has a definite impact on where you are going to be five years from now.

(2) **Your goals must be worthwhile.** You must believe that your goal has value. It should also be something that makes you enthusiastic. The key to all discipline is desire; the more you desire something, the easier self-discipline becomes. Life-goals enable you to filter out everything else and concentrate all your energies and resources in a single direction.

(3) **Your goals should be clear-cut.** The more specific a goal, the better your chances of reaching it.

People who set definitive goals make things happen. People who set unclear goals end up waiting for something to happen. People who don't set goals spend most of their lives wondering what happened!

(4) **Your goals need a timetable.** If you want to start getting somewhere, set specific goals, give yourself definite deadlines for reaching them, then hold yourself to those deadlines. Unless you write your goals and timetables, you probably aren't serious about reaching them.

(5) **You must be true to your goals.** A goal is a pledge to yourself, but most of us are a lot better at keeping the promises we make to others than we are at keeping the promises we make to ourselves. Maybe that is the

reason other people always seem to have more confidence in us than we have in ourselves.

Goals only work when we consider them to be promises we make to ourselves, and keep them with the same tenacity with which we would keep a promise to our dearest loved ones.

(6) **Goals should cover every segment of your life.** Many people fail to reap the full benefit of setting goals because they confine them to their business careers.

For example, some of the most outstanding entertainment, civic, business and political leaders are complete failures in relationships with family members. Likewise, some college professors have marvelous minds, yet they completely ignore their need for physical fitness.

A good set of goals covers every area of life: career growth, family life, social development, mental-physical-spiritual well-being, financial security--every aspect which you feel is important.

(7) **Your goals should be stepping stones to higher goals.** An achiever's mindset should cause you to keep evaluating and extending your goals. You must keep expanding your horizons.

And what happens if you don't fulfill your goals? I remember one backwoods preacher who used to say, "It's better to shoot for the moon and hit the picket fence than to aim for the fence and hit the ground!" If you give it your best shot, you will have the deep inner satisfaction of knowing you tried. Like most goal-setters, you will probably double your efforts and keep going. More importantly, you will be miles ahead of where you would have been otherwise.

When your plan is well-defined, properly-pursued goals and dreams direct your life toward positive achievement. No one can set these for you, since they are a personal matter. Each must set his or her own goals and build toward them day by day, week by week, month by month and year by year.

Success is the progressive realization of a worthwhile goal. The goals you set, then, are extremely important.

ACTION PLAN

Your vision and values are the basis for your dream list. Your dreams form the foundation for the goals you set. Those goals, then, become the springboard for your action plan.

A strong action plan--most importantly your daily, weekly and monthly steps, but also including your yearly schedule--when carefully written and consistently followed, can lead eventually to the attainment of your ideals. All else--your vision, dreams and goals--will be lost unless you add the fourth element, **action**!

What about your plan of action?

Take a few moments and write a statement about what your life could be like in five years, providing you continue living as you are right now. Remember to cover all the areas of life which are important to you.

Then, write a sentence or two detailing the changes you would like to make in your life during the next five years in each of the important areas.

Finally, what are the key strategies you will need to use to make those changes?

DECISIONS

You hold the key to tomorrow's doors. Your actions and decisions affect all the next steps. You see, dreams are a little like riding through a prosperous neighborhood and trying to imagine living in one of the most beautiful homes you see. Setting goals is like picking out one of those homes, and promising yourself you will have one just like it (except for the few personal changes you would like to make) by a certain date.

But, if that is all that ever happens, you will only wind up frustrated. You might even come to resent the people who "have the good fortune" to live in those fabulous houses. In addition to having dreams and goals, you must also develop a concrete plan to make your aspirations come true. You have to become a practical dreamer.

Dr. David J. Schwartz, author of *The Magic of Thinking Big* said it best many times in speeches and interviews: "Persons who reach the top rungs in business management, selling, engineering, religious work, writing, acting, and in every other pursuit get there by following conscientiously and continuously a plan for self-development and growth."

Your action plan and subsequent activities will never be any better than the goals on which they are based. Therefore, let me encourage you to set aside a definite time during the next few days to formulate a complete set of goals for every area of your life. Start with long-range goals, then break them down into intermediate and short-range goals.

Whether you vision is to climb Mount Everest, run for political office, lose ten pounds, go on a missions trip to some remote area of the world, run a marathon, build a million-dollar business or wind up in the corner office, you must put together a formulated, step-by-step process. Your dreams must be broken in pieces small enough to conquer them one by one.

HAL GOOCH ♦ *STREET SMARTS* ♦ Proverb 5♦ 10

Now, what do you want to do in the next five years? How are you going to reach those goals? What is your action plan?

Proverb 6
"Bend or break."

"Flexibility is the key to success. In today's fast-paced world, flexibility is an absolute requirement for survival. Having only one unbending action plan is risky. To survive today, you must be able to change with the times. Otherwise, you are like a football team with only one play—it may work once or twice, but the opposing team is going to catch on."

THE BULLRING

Old Spanish proverb: "No es lo mismo hablar de toros, que estar en el redondel."

English translation: "It's not the same to talk of bulls as to be in the bullring."

STREET SMARTS application: You will never know how successful you can be until you have been in the business "bullring."

There is an old military axiom that says, "No battle plan survives contact with the enemy." As discussed in Proverb 5, goals and a detailed action plan are important to your success. But you cannot be a slave to a paper plan. When you face whatever comes against you in the "bullring" of life, flexibility is the key. Critical adjustments in the midst of the proverbial battle are vital to long-term success.

SUCCESS DEFINED

What is success? I know that there are numerous definitions of success. Earl Nightingale's statement has been quoted around the world: "Success is the progressive realization of a worthwhile goal."

I've learned this quote many years ago: "Success is not the reverse of failure; it is the scorn of failure. Always dare to fail; never fail to dare."

Here are several more that I have gleaned:

Norman Vincent Peale: "Success comes from mastering defeat."

Former heavyweight boxing champion Joe Louis: "Success consists of getting up just one more time than you fell down."

Masterful inventor Booker T. Washington: "Success is not measured by the heights one attains, but by the obstacles one overcomes in their attainment."

Christopher Morley: "There is only one success--to be able to spend your life in your own way."

I like those quotes and definitions, but let me offer you the most simple, six-word equation of success that you will find:

STARTING

+ BEING

+ DOING

+ OVERCOMING

+ FLEXIBILITY

= SUCCESS

These ideas are mainly given as springboards for your own creative thoughts. Let's quickly go through each part of the equation:

HAL GOOCH ♦ *STREET SMARTS* ♦ Proverb 6 ♦ 4

☐ **STARTING:** I've heard many people say, "Ninety percent of success is showing up." That isn't totally true, but there is a lesson in the words. You can't get anywhere without starting. Many people are content to talk about their dreams, but you must be willing to get up and start putting one foot in front of the other.

☐ **BEING:** No matter what happens, learn to enjoy the journey. Henry David Thoreau wrote, "If one advances confidently in the direction of his dreams, and endeavors to live the life which he has imagined, he will meet with a success unexpected in common hours."

☐ **DOING:** No rule for success will work if you won't! The secret of success for every person who is, or has ever been successful, lies in the fact that he or she has formed the habit of doing things that failures don't like to do.

☐ **OVERCOMING:** Charles Kettering, chief executive for many years with General Motors, often said, "Ninety-nine percent of success is built on former failure." Success comes from mastering defeat.

☐ **FLEXIBILITY:** You will face challenges on your road to success. You will have to go from Plan A to Plan B. You will have to improvise while smiling on the outside and feeling sheer terror on the inside. John Ruskin wrote: "The successful man lengthens his stride when he discovers the signpost has deceived him; the failure looks for a place to sit down." Flexibility is the key.

- **SUCCESS:** "Success is simple," said oft-quoted Bunker Hunt, the Texas Billionaire. "First, you decide exactly what you want in life. Second, you decide whether you are willing to pay the price to make it happen--and then you pay the price."

You are on a journey. The difference between success and failure will continue to be decided by how you handle both everyday and watershed events. Experience, no matter what happens, is still one of the best teachers.

FLEXIBILITY ADJUSTMENTS

You cannot control what other people do. You cannot control every element of your action plan—remember "The best laid plans of mice and men…?" The only thing you have control over is how you motivate yourself as you face both bad and good circumstances. The way you control your attitude is the best way to bend, but not break, when life is filled with barriers.

Let me suggest five practical strategies for **bending, not breaking**, as you commit yourself to make positive things happen in every area of your life:

HAL GOOCH ♦ STREET SMARTS ♦ Proverb 6 ♦ 6

(1) **A positive day starts the night before**, so spend time each night reflecting on the good things that have happened that day. Lay out your clothes. Check "to do" lists for the next day.

John D. Rockefeller's habit of ended each day was well known. He said that he always emptied his pockets very slowly, the last thing before he retired. As he took things out of his pockets, he made a conscious effort to empty his mind of all worry, anxiety and negative thoughts.

(2) **Begin each day positively.** The most important hour in each day is often the first hour you are awake. That first hour sets the pace for the remainder of the day. Starting out the day on a positive note sets a tone for being able to handle everything that happens.

(3) **Keep your goals constantly in front of you.** I've shared ways for you to develop dreams, goals and an action plan, but your aspirations are only as good as the way they are focused in your mind. Visualize yourself reaching your goals and replay that mental picture. Then, no matter what arises, you will be able to keep your sense of direction.

(4) **Keep reminding yourself why you want to succeed.** One millionaire has been asked many times why he succeeded when people he grew up with never made it. His simple answer is: "I guess I just had more reasons to get rich than they did."

What are your reasons for succeeding? Are you willing to spend time each day concentrating on those reasons? One of the best ways to keep yourself motivated is to focus as many reasons as you can think of to succeed, and to keep reminding yourself of all those reasons.

(5) **Be flexible even in the area of criticism.** Remember, success invites criticism. Learn what you can from feedback of friends, business associates and certainly the competition. Change what you should.

It simply is not practical to think that you can achieve anything in life without experiencing the barbs of criticism and disappointment. However, when those stinging comments come, remind yourself that you are in excellent company! Anyone who has ever succeeded in anything has felt the stinging darts from jealous and misunderstanding people. The only way to avoid criticism is to say nothing, do nothing and be nothing!

Above all, don't be surprised or shocked when challenges happen to you. Barriers and course-corrections are normal. No one is the best at everything all the time. By definition, you **cannot** succeed unless you encounter challenges. Sometimes you will fail, perhaps miserably. But the greatest question is not, "Will I keep getting knocked down?" but "Will I keep getting up?"

HAL GOOCH ♦ *STREET SMARTS* ♦ Proverb 6 ♦ 8

BEND OR BREAK CHAMPIONS

The record books are filled with stories about people who failed time and again, but ultimately succeeded:

☐ **Babe Ruth** held the record for strike-outs long before he set the homerun record. The "Sultan of Swat" Babe once said, "I may have my faults, but givin' up ain't one of `em."

☐ **Henry Ford** became the "Father of Mass Production" with his immensely popular automobiles. The Model T, brought out in 1908, had sales of 10,607 the first year. In four years sales jumped to 168,304, and in four more, to 730,041. During Model T's lifetime, 1908-1927, production added up to 15,458,781 cars -- more than the total of all other cars produced collectively by all other American and foreign auto makers during those years. It has been called "the most widely used vehicle in human history." Still, Ford forgot a reverse gear in his first car. Later, the "Father of Mass Production" said, "I always learn more from my failures than from my successes."

☐ **Thomas Edison** is history's most prodigious inventor and developer of new products, most notably the incandescent light bulb and phonograph. The United States Patent Office granted him 1,098 patents during his lifetime, 122 of them before he was 30 years of age. But he also was known to spend as much as $2 million on one invention that proved of little value. Edison tried thousands of materials before he found the one that made his incandescent light work. In the midst of his marathon effort, one of his assistants complained, "Mr. Edison, we have already tried five hundred experiments without a solution to the problem in sight. We are trying but we aren't getting results." Edison smiled, "My friend, we do have results. We now know five hundred ways that will not work!"

Many successful people had mediocre talents, most struggled against overwhelming odds and all had many reasons to give up. But they kept going, despite the losses, until they overcame the odds. They kept bending, not breaking, until they overcame the problems.

`YO, ROCKY

Who can forget the make-it-or-break-it moment in the first Sylvester Stallone ROCKY movie? His face is swollen and bloody, is opponent has knocked him to the canvas over and over, and yet—DING! CUE THE MUSIC!—as the noise builds before the bell that begins the final round, Rocky proclaims, "I ain't goin' down no more!"

Needless to say, Rocky bent, but didn't break. Well, that is, unless you count his nose! Seriously, will you be flexible—DING! CUE THE MUSIC!--no matter what happens? Can you simply refuse to stay down? Can you focus on results, not on problems? Will you be able to keep yourself motivated? Can you sustain your commitment to making good things happen, even when you have reached Plan Z?

HAL GOOCH ♦ *STREET SMARTS* ♦ Proverb 6 ♦ 10

To be an outstanding success in any endeavor, it is not necessary to be right all the time. If you are right more than half the time, you may win a gold medal, make a million dollars, invent a new computer program, build a huge business organization, develop a cure for a dreaded disease or join the top 5% of your industry.

The idea is to keep doing the things that successful people do. Be flexible. Develop a positive attitude that will override anything that occurs. Commit yourself to making things happen—to bending, not breaking—in the bullring of life!

Proverb 7
"Check and re-check."

"No matter how good they say you are, always keep working on your game."

Michael Jordan
Six-time National Basketball Association Champion Chicago Bulls and Finals MVP Each Year; Olympic "Dream Team" Gold Medalist

CHANGES

The remarkable Tiger Woods did something even more remarkable, right after the 1997 season. During that season he joined the pro tour at age 20, won four of the 15 PGA Tour tournaments, earned $1.8-million in prize money and over $60 million in Nike and Titleist endorsements. In short, he captivated the game as no rookie ever had. After he ended the season by dominating the Masters Tournament (eventually winning by a whopping 12 strokes against the best golfers in the world), he could have deservedly taken a long vacation in preparation for another assault on the record books during 1998.

Not Tiger. He carefully studied videotapes of his performances. To everyone else, including most golfing insiders, he looked almost unbeatable as he blasted 300-yard drives from the tee, hit stunningly accurate iron shots down the fairway and drained putts from anywhere on any green.

Tiger called his coach, Butch Harmon, and told him he wanted to make some serious changes to his swing. That's not new—lots of great golfers have attempted to revamp their game. Most, however, were past their prime. Few, if any, ever returned to earlier glory. What was Tiger Woods thinking?

In a mid-2000 interview with *TIME* Magazine, Woods recalled: "I knew I wasn't in the greatest positions in my swing at the Masters, but my timing was great, so I got away with it. And I made almost every putt. You can have a wonderful week like that even when your swing isn't sound. But can you still contend in tournaments with that swing when your timing isn't as good? Will it hold up over a long period of time? The answer to those questions, with the swing I had, was no. And I wanted to change that."

Tiger Woods based his decision on checking, viewing video, asking lots of questions, and re-checking. Those steps are always wise in any profession or enterprise. But the dramatic course correction Tiger decided to take was a huge risk. Such huge risks can be disastrous.

And how did Tiger's checking, re-checking and course corrections turn out? Slowly, at first. He won only one Tour event during the 19 months between July 1997 and February 1999. Each time he lost, he declared that he was "a better golfer" than when he was winning in early 1997. "Winning," he was quoted, "is not always the barometer of getting better." Woods says he first knew he was coming out of the tunnel on a cool evening in May 1999 on the practice ground at the gated Isleworth community where he lives, outside Orlando, Fla. He phoned his coach with the words, "I think I'm back."

And the victories came. He won an extraordinary 10 of 14 events during the rest of 1999 and had eight PGA Tour victories in that year, the most since Johnny Miller in 1974. The onslaught has continued to the point that many agree with professional golfer Ernie Els: "The rest of us are playing one tournament, and then there's Tiger, playing a different one."

COURSE CORRECTIONS

No one is perfect. In the marketing world, people make mistakes and bad course corrections because they misjudge the public. But it gets a bit more complicated when the need for monitoring and course corrections becomes personal. Many people fail, to use a cliché, because they can't see the "forest" for the "trees."

Mistakes and errors of judgement are a valuable part of life, for in them we find another reason to keep dreaming, no matter what happens. The attitude we take toward mistakes and failures, separates the successful person from the unsuccessful man or woman.

Coco Channel failed in her first efforts to find the perfect perfume. It took Channel No. 5 to do the trick. Likewise, chemist Paul Ehrlich discovered a drug to treat people who were afflicted with syphilis. It was named "Formula 606" because the first 605 tests had been unsuccessful. Another man was viewed as a mild lunatic by most railroad executives when he suggested that a train could be stopped by using wind. Yet George Westinghouse persevered and finally sold what is now the Westinghouse Air Brake, a standard feature on American trains.

When successful people fail, they think about what went wrong and what they can do differently the next time. Frankly, most of us can deal with success. However, what we do when we make mistakes is the one thing that determines what we get out of life.

You should know that it does not matter how many mistakes you make, or even how many times you fail on your road to success. What matters is the concentrated attempt to learn from each failure and to improve performance the next time around. What you need to do is use that information to make better decisions about what you need to do to produce whatever results you ultimately desire. Granted, you may be allowed fewer and fewer mistakes as you move up the success ladder, but you can never reach the point where you stop taking risks.

Make mistakes, but never allow yourself to stay wallowed in your misery. You must be creative, not reactive. Strength only comes through life's lessons and character building. Say to yourself, "How can I make something good come out of this?"

Here are four course corrections that will help you overcome your failures or judgement errors:

☐ **LEARN FROM EXPERIENCE**

If you are unable to be taught by the past, you will be condemned to repeat it. When you fail, attempt to determine what caused that failure. Likewise, when you succeed, seek to understand what you did to produce positive results. As simplistic as it may seem, success is simply learning what does and does not work. There's no reason to beat yourself up emotionally when you make bad judgements. Resolve to learn all you can from your experiences.

☐ **SEEK COACHES TO MONITOR AND GUIDE**

In many instances, the best teacher is a mentor or coach who has the experience to help you make wise course corrections. The top sports professionals pay millions of dollars to coaches who carefully check everything to see if good habits are unknowingly being replaced by bad ones. The best corporations in the world hire well-paid consultants to monitor each part of these organizations and make recommendations for change. So, why do we think it is so difficult or unusual to have coaches and mentors in our lives to help us check vital signs and offer suggestions for success?

☐ **AIM HIGH**

You've probably already noticed that many of the Proverbs in STREET SMARTS deal with your dreams and goals. The reason should always be clear: Your goals make the difference between aimless wandering and effective action, especially as a businessperson, and specifically when you need to make course corrections. It's hard to make good course corrections while you are drifting around haphazardly.

☐ **CONCENTRATE ON PRODUCTIVE EFFORT.**

A song written back in the Sixties had this line: "Life is what happens to you while you're busy making other plans." I've found that most people spend the majority of their time aimlessly, merely doing busywork, as they wait for the "big" moments in life. For you to be successful in making course corrections, you must focus on effective efforts all the time, even when the spotlight isn't focused on you.

☐ **KEEP MOVING**

As part of monitoring your progress and making course corrections, it's important to keep setting new goals and dreams for yourself. Most people don't quit on life deliberately, but they give up their visions a piece at a time when they run into barriers or detours. Determine over and over what success means to you, then do whatever is necessary to make the changes to achieve your dreams.

No one else has as great a stake in your future and your family's future as you do, so monitoring your progress is crucial to them, as well. Seek their input. Ask, don't tell. Build your vision with them, not just your business colleagues. And when you have to make course corrections, don't leave them groping around without your encouragement. More than ever, you need your family and close friends during times of change.

GOOD JUDGEMENT

A successful man was asked the secret of his accomplishments. His reply was: "Good judgement."

"Where did you learn good judgement," he was asked.

"From experience."

"And where did you gain your experience?"

"From bad judgement!"

It's not always true that you have to learn from experience. You can discover many ways to succeed through the experiences of others. Somehow, though, you must be able to check and re-check throughout your life. Then, when needed, make course corrections to change your life for the better.

Proverb 8
"You can't get far on empty."

"I made an analogy once of a plane going down and people jettisoning all the weight to keep the plane up. I think one of the first things to go as people's lives start to go down is their dreams. Dreams should be the last thing to go--dreams are things you go down with. If you're left clinging to a piece of driftwood in the middle of the ocean, I'd put on it the word dreams."

Kevin Costner
Motion Picture Actor and Director

HAL GOOCH ♦ *STREET SMARTS* ♦ Proverb 8 ♦ 2

THE EGG

One day, quite by accident, a farmer found an eagle's egg on a hill. He carried it to his chicken coop and placed it beside some eggs in a hen's nest. The hen, not knowing the difference, covered the egg with her wings and protected it for its incubation period. Soon, the eagle hatched among a brood of prairie chickens. As it grew up it mimicked the actions of the other chickens. It learned to cluck, scratch and bob when it walked. It flapped its wings to fly a few feet in the air. It ate seeds and insects. It had no reason to believe it was not a prairie chicken.

One day the little eagle looked up in the sky and saw the most majestic creature it had ever seen soaring in wide circles. "What is that?" it asked in awe.

"That," said a nearby prairie chicken, "is an eagle, the greatest of all birds."

"That's what I want to be!" exclaimed the eagle.

You're crazy," exclaimed the field hen. "You can't be an eagle. You're a chicken."

So, the little eaglet hung its head and began scratching the ground. "I guess you're right."

From that moment and throughout its entire life, the eagle continued living among the chickens, not knowing what kind of potential it had, not knowing it was born to soar. It never even tried to fly higher than a few feet or eat different food. It was convinced that it was impossible. And, when the eagle died, it died a prairie chicken.

A lot of people die prairie chickens because they have given up on their "childish," "foolish" dreams. Sure, they may have thought at one time that they could achieve great things amidst the most incredible odds. But what happened? How many people do you know who are content, so to speak, to spend a lifetime scratching the ground and nibbling at bugs?

EIGHT REASONS FOR DREAMS

Too many people are caught in dreamless, prairie chicken lives. The dream, or the cause for your goals, must constantly be revisited. Inspiration is the fuel; if you run out, your engine will eventually stop. Let's look quickly at eight reasons why you must continually go back to your dreams to avoid running on empty:

- REASON 1: DREAMS CREATE HOPE

Many of us are so wrapped up in the struggle of surviving that we act like zombies going through the routine of life. Consequently, we become discontented and complacent. Dreams provide the ability for people to look beyond life's struggles. They enable us to rise above the ordinary.

Dreams help us differentiate between how things are and how we want them to be. They allow us to shift our thinking from the negative to the positive. In other words, dreams create hope. Human beings are constantly searching for the meaning of life. The act of dreaming can help us discover depths in ourselves that we never knew existed.

The thrill in living is tied up with our hopes and dreams. Hope makes life an adventure. It lifts us and makes good things happen.

☐ REASON 2: DREAMS CALL US TO GREATNESS

Have you ever noticed how dreams often call people to be more than they thought they could be--to run faster, to climb higher, to think more creatively, to work more effectively and to win against all odds?

George Frideric Handel tapped into it. When he composed *The Messiah*, he worked 24 days straight with no sleep and little food. He was driven to perfect what was to become one of the most famous musical scores ever written. How did he do it? His dream called him to greatness, for it gave him a tremendous burst of power and stamina.

Dreams are supposed to do that. Bear in mind, however, that dreams don't really encourage us to accomplish the impossible. Actually, dreams merely show us what is possible.

☐ REASON 3: DREAMS MAKE THE UNBEARABLE BEARABLE

How many dream-shatterers can you take before you are ruined? Do you give up when your dreams are accompanied by suffering? Harry Emerson Fosdick once wrote: "Life doesn't ask simply how much can you do, but how much can you take without being spoiled by it." There are plenty of reasons to be "spoiled." Life doles out unbearable situations to everyone, in varying amounts. The key to overcoming these challenges is learning how to tolerate circumstances without letting them ruin us. The best way to do that? Dream! Dreams give people something to live for by establishing goals worth striving for. Human beings must always be reaching beyond their grasps. Otherwise it becomes too easy to give up.

Ask Joni Erickson Tada, paralyzed as a teenager from the neck down through a diving accident. She will quickly start talking about her dreams. The results are clear-cut, since she has become an accomplished painter (she holds the brush in her teeth), author (her books have sold into the millions) and much-in-demand speaker.

☐ REASON 4: DREAMS GIVE PERSPECTIVE IN CHALLENGES

When life seems futile, intolerable or useless, dreams can help us keep things in perspective. In other words, they can give meaning to a person's present sufferings.

HAL GOOCH ♦ STREET SMARTS ♦ Proverb 8 ♦ 6

Most people can withstand unimaginable hardships and deal with setbacks much easier if they have a dream constantly in focus.

Vietnam POWs such as Everett Alvarez, Jr., Bobby Begley and Jeremiah Denton are examples. By clinging to their dreams they kept life in perspective. They focused on returning to normal life, being with their families or reaching a goal, whether it was to play the best golf game ever or start a business. They forced themselves to dream; otherwise they could not have endured the suffering.

Some POWs, as Alvarez mentioned in his book, *Chained Eagle*, formed Toastmasters Clubs. Others, as both Begley and Denton described in their books, memorized long passages of the Bible from pieced-together Scriptures and learned how to play the guitar or piano by practicing on mental musical instruments.

Though I have certainly never experienced anything like being chained in a North Vietnamese prison, I know very well that if I had not focused on a dream many years ago when starting out as a business owner, I would have easily lost my way.

☐ REASON 5: DREAMS PROVIDE ENERGY FOR ACHIEVEMENT

Dreams fuel a sense of purpose in our lives. Purpose gives a mission, an objective in life. Most people don't have purpose without having a dream. The two go hand-in-hand.

Henry Ford had a dream. He wanted to create an automobile the average person could afford. That dream established a sense of purpose in his life: He wanted to put America on wheels. And, he did. Because of a dream-led purpose in life, Ford initiated the mass-transportation explosion.

When we allow dreams to be a part of our lives, we energize ourselves in ways we never thought possible. We receive the direction we need to achieve success. Dreams help us determine what avenues to take in life, what goals to pursue.

REASON 6: DREAMS CAUSE EXCITEMENT

When people are sold out 100% to achieving a particular goal, they get excited. If you have ever been involved in any sport, you know what I am saying.

I live within an hour of Duke University, North Carolina State and the University of North Carolina. Any basketball fan understands the excitement you feel when the "Blue Devils," "Wolfpack" or "Tarheels" run onto the court. The roar shakes you to the core. Even the most restrained people get caught up in such contagious, exhilarating moments. When a national ranking or a conference championship are on the line, the intensity is unbelievable. That excitement ignites a fire that spreads throughout the fans, and no words can adequately describe how it feels. That can happen in your life and in your business when your dreams get big enough.

REASON 7: DREAMS GIVE SELF-WORTH

Have you ever felt like you didn't have any worthwhile identity or self-value? Maybe it has seemed as if you have lived your life trying to make others happy or striving for the goals that others had set for you. I certainly have. But, I learned that dreaming could release me from that. Each of us has a unique mind, and our dreams are equally unique. Never give up your dreams by default. There is a wonderful exhilaration that comes when you realize that you can think your own thoughts. Dreams give self-worth.

REASON 8: DREAMS BUILD SELF-CONFIDENCE

Probably the most significant positive affect of dreaming is not just self-worth, but self-confidence. People with big dreams act confidently on the foundation of self-worth. In fact, only the people who are willing to risk dreaming are willing to risk failure. And, as discussed in Proverb 7, each course correction is one step closer to success.

NO MORE EMPTY DREAM-TANKS

Can you remember a time when you were so motivated to do something that nothing could stand in your way? I am amazed at students who are so driven to earn their college degrees that they carry heavy class-loads, work 40 hours a week, remain involved socially and still maintain outstanding grade point averages.

Dreams ignite those sparks residing deep inside us all and fan them into consuming flames. When those flames start burning, they create unquenchable passions. They inspire, as the Army slogan reminds, to help us "BE ALL THAT YOU CAN BE!" Dreams call us to greatness.

Big dreams enable us to operate beyond normal capacity. But, most of us just don't know how to tap into that power. You have heard stories about people who lift cars and do other extraordinary feats of physical power to save their loved ones. Where do they get this strength? Medically, this power is tied to a surge of adrenaline. But, there is more to it. In crises, people can reach deep into themselves and take advantage of a dormant, untouched power. That power is inspired by dreams.

Life is what you make it, and what you make it depends upon your dreams. What do you want to be? What are you willing to do to reach your goals? When you find the answer to those questions, you simultaneously discover the secret to avoid for running out of fuel. Are you ready for that?

Proverb 9
"A lone wolf eventually starves."

*"If you want one year of prosperity, grow grain.
If you want ten years of prosperity, grow trees.
If you want one hundred years of prosperity,
grow people."*

--CHINESE PROVERB

HAL GOOCH ♦ *STREET SMARTS* ♦ Proverb 9 ♦ 2

THE LONE WOLF

The lone wolf is such a popular figure in music, drama and folk culture. He's the lobo, the go-it-alone guy, the pilgrim, the solitary man. Who of us didn't grow up loving the lone wolf in movies? You remember the John Wayne-James Dean-Clint Eastwood-Richard Roundtree-Bruce Willis types? They were the ones who stood silhouetted against the world, defied all odds, those lone heroes who asked for no quarter and received none as they overcame injustice, then rode into the sunset. During the past couple of decades, more women, too, have popularized this anti-hero type on the big screen, television serials and recordings.

In life, it's true that you must be able to dream your own dreams, chart your own course and stand on your own feet. However, it is a myth to believe that you can achieve or sustain any measurable level of success by yourself. Especially if you desire to do anything great in life, there are only three ways to get anything done:

- ☐ **Do it yourself.**
- ☐ **Get help.**
- ☐ **Give help.**

You can build very little going it yourself as a lone wolf. To get help and give help, it is necessary to learn team-building skills. Your success as a businessperson, in fact, will depend almost completely on how effective you are in getting people to help you achieve common goals.

TEAMWORK IN A DOT.COM WORLD

Jim Clark has been called a lone wolf, but in reality he is far from it. Who is he? If you don't know, you are probably not living in the dot.com world. Not everyone has three multi-billion-dollar start-ups under their belt. Jim Clark has. As co-founder of Netscape, Silicon Graphics and Healtheon, he has built business teams that thrive in the dot.com world. This internet pioneer is a self-made multibillionaire rewriting the rules of American business. He took the notion of the top-down, hierarchical organization and almost single-handedly made it obsolete.

"It just comes down to leadership," he has said several times. "It comes from a combination of being persuasive; believing in what you're doing; having integrity and knowing how to judge good people as you build your team, because you can't afford to have anything but good people early on in a company or organization."

Pioneering risky and ground-breaking startup internet companies has required him to lay a foundation of innovative professionals. Clark says that all have to be talented and pull their own weight. Otherwise—disaster! So how does he build great teams?

"I look for intelligence and a certain measure of humility," Clark admits candidly. "People who are boastful or too proud may be really good, but they're not my kind of people."

Clark also chooses team-members who are willing to listen and understand what the other people on the team have to offer. Says the multibillionaire entrepreneur, "A business is about teams, and teams mean getting along with people. There's just not enough room for a lot of super-egos in a company."

Few leaders inspire more devotion from their employees than Clark does. And he'll insist it has little to do with charisma or a brilliant capacity for computer technology. Success simply starts with team-building.

"Companies aren't built by individuals, they are built by teams of people," Clark has said in interviews. "They are like a tribe of people with a common set of goals and—to the extent that you can have all the people honestly contribute—you make them a part of the process. You make them a shareholder. You make them win when the company wins. I think those are the really important aspects of companies and organizations as we create them today."

Most people agree that today's dot.com world has little room for the lone wolf. But then, that has always been the case. Truly great projects, projects that last, demand lost of dedicated people, including some with great, specialized talents. So how do you begin building your team?

TEAMWORK

Working together is sometimes one of the hardest things most of us ever do. It gets easier, of course, as the bonds of trust grow and as we begin seeing the benefits. But it is often difficult to work together in a democratic manner.

The "hardest thing?" you might say. "How hard can team-building be?" After all, we all know the importance of working together, right?"

It's true that we've been flooded with "If-we-all-pull-together" songs and messages since childhood. Super Bowl quarterbacks smile into television cameras and say, "I couldn't have thrown that winning pass without my offensive line--they are the real heroes." Olympic medallists laud their coaches and the encouragement of the crowd.

The team concept is important. Teamwork is essential for any organization or company to be productive. Teamwork is needed to develop mutual commitment. It's not just a good-sounding cliché. Teamwork, quite simply, is vital. It is the one thing that leaders can develop to unlock the creativity, skills and talents available throughout their organization.

If teamwork is the "key, how then do you unlock these forces. The answer?

LEVERAGE

Archimedes once said, "Give me a lever and I can move the world." Leverage is the most powerful when used with people. Leverage is also the key to understanding teamwork.

The late J. Paul Getty, one of the richest men in history, once said, "If you help enough people get what they want, you will automatically get what you want."

Learning the value of leverage is one of the most important concepts you will discover. At the same time, getting people to work with you is more than a quick-fix; it is, in fact, one of the toughest character-building exercises you will ever experience. If you want to be an integral part of any team, you need to become the best YOU.

As you forge a better YOU, you must begin to build your team. If you have not built a network of friends and co-workers--people who rely on you, with whom you can trust vital information and to whom you can turn to in times of crisis--you are missing a key ingredient in the strategy of people-leveraging.

In business, on an athletic field, in politics and at home, you need a lot of people, spread out in the right places, whom you can depend on (and vice-versa). A network is not something that can be established overnight. Your network will require nurturing, but you must develop a strong, supportive group of co-workers and friends.

A network is a mutually helpful, flexible group of associates and friends. You cannot build that structure easily. You must be willing to give much more than you get. Or as Dale Carnegie often said, "You can make more friends in two months by becoming interested in other people than you can in two years by trying to get people interested in you." Just remember--networking amplifies your development as a team-builder.

THREE BASIC TEAM-BUILDING GUIDELINES

So how do you begin to network with others to build your team? First, it is important to recognize the three corps elements of a successful team:

(1)   A Common Objective

With a common objective, everyone wins or loses. It requires uncommon amounts of cohesiveness for this to happen. The key to a common objective is sharing a powerful dream. It means being willing to forego your own purposes for the good of the team. It means becoming a master at helping others to develop their own dreams.

(2) Meaningful giving and taking

This requires honesty, openness and trust. It necessitates a high degree of integrity on the part of everyone involved. It is built on sharing thoughts and ideas candidly. It may even mean confronting without being angry. One warning: You can have a common objective without having to interact in a meaningful way. Meaningful interaction means moving deeper than merely having a common objective; it means probing a heartfelt relationship as a team.

(3) Mutual Commitment

Rather than remaining a collection of individuals (Anytime two or more are together, you are a team--remember?), identity and commitment require heart and personal responsibility on the part of everyone who is involved.

If you decide to do something great--something that will impact your world--you will need others. You will need mentors, friends, advisors, accountants, lawyers, salespersons, managers, counselors, manufacturers, wholesalers, retailers, technicians and so many more. In any of these relationships, conflict will eventually erupt unless you have a common objective, meaningful interaction and mutual commitment.

Actually, it appears that there are many advantages running the show by yourself. You have no board or stockholders or committees to whom you must answer. You have supreme flexibility. You can act quickly, making course corrections in an instant. But these advantages are often deceiving. A lone wolf in today's economy will soon starve to death.

HORIZONS

Remember, as I mentioned in the beginning of this proverb, there are only three ways to get anything done:

- ☐ **Do it yourself.**
- ☐ **Get help.**
- ☐ **Give help.**

Each of those ways is good, but each is also limiting. Studies have shown that those who achieve outstanding success have generally done so by expanding and leveraging their efforts through others—by doing all three ways simultaneously.

If you want to have a profound impact in the game of life, develop the ability to believe and invest yourself in others. If you do, people will return your gift a thousand times.

Proverb 10
*"Be a wise old owl...
listen your way to success."*

"A wise old owl sat on an oak;
the more he saw, the less he spoke;
the less he spoke, the more he heard;
God make me more
like that wise old owl."

--Nursery Rhyme

THE TEAM-BUILDING KEY

So you want to build a great team of achievers? Whether you are recruiting a sales force, encouraging your family or overseeing a multi-national organization, the key to building your team is listening, not merely telling. It means overcoming barriers. It includes asking the right kind of questions. Mostly, it means using your listening skills to discovering solutions for everyone involved.

Imagine how life would be if doctors acted as many businesspeople do? You might walk into a doctor's office one day and be greeted with a scenario like this:

"I fell and hurt my left arm," you begin. "I don't think it's broken, but it might be sprained or something."

"Your arm? Boy, are you in luck today!" the doctor says, smiling broadly.

"I don't feel so lucky," you respond. "It hurts like crazy!"

"You know *why* this is your lucky day?" the physician asks hungrily, totally ignoring your comment. "We're running an incredible close-out sale on artificial limbs . . .we're getting ready for the new models!"

HAL GOOCH ♦ *STREET SMARTS* ♦ Proverb 10 ♦ 3

"Doc'" you protest, "My arm hurts, but I don't need an artificial limb, for cryin' out loud!"

"What better time than now?" he continues talking smoothly, "I can fix you up with this `Arnold Schwartzenagger' model! It's just like the one the big guy used in his latest movie—TERMINATOR XII--the flick where he plays yet another alien robot. This baby is loaded with options, and you can get it, today only, for the unbelievably low price of $100,000! That's a savings of nearly $25,000. Don't you agree that this is an incredible deal?"

The doctor nods gently until you acknowledge positively, then he adds, "Besides, it's all covered by your insurance. Look at the muscles ripple on that baby! Could I schedule you for installation Tuesday, or would Thursday be more convenient for you?"

You would RUN, not walk, to the nearest exit!

BECOME A "MATLOCK"

The story about the doctor and his "Arnold Schwartzanegger'" artificial arm is fictitious, or is it? Businesspeople and team-builder wannabes who subscribe to this "jawbone theory" (some call it the "shotgun theory") of building organizations often lose out because they focus more on what NUMBER ONE wants to happen than on what the other person desires.

HAL GOOCH ♦ *STREET SMARTS* ♦ Proverb 10 ♦ 4

You can overcome this lethal weakness by learning to question and listen well. You must look beneath the surface to discover and reveal what is going on in the person's mind and heart. You must become a MATLOCK!

Now, for those readers who don't remember one of television's best programs, let me brag for a moment on a program that was largely filmed in eastern North Carolina, not far from my home. Tarheel native son Andy Griffith played the role of Matlock. The premise of every show was basically the same: By the first commercial break, the audience already had a good idea who committed the crime. The only one who didn't seem to know is the lead character.

The coolest part was that Matlock didn't use high-pressure tactics. He simply spent the rest of the program getting people to trust him and finally open up. He had to be cool. He was a lawyer. Of course, actor Andy Griffith didn't even wear a gun when he played Sheriff Andy Taylor back in Mayberry! Throughout each Matlock program he remained non-threatening. He kept asking questions. If he didn't get enough information with one question, he rephrased the same inquiry in another way:

"I'm just curious. . ."

"Could you help me out with this?"

"Just one more thing. . ."

"Can we go over this again so I can understand?"

Before the final commercial break, bam! Matlock would strike again and another criminal would be led off in chains.

Bottom line? To succeed at business and team-building, you have to become a Matlock-like master at asking questions.

QUESTION YOUR WAY TO SUCCESS

The single-most valuable tool of the businessperson is the skillfully asked question. The right query at the right time will enable you to do three very important things:

- ☐ **Questions permit you to discover what the other person wants and the conditions upon which he or she would be willing to buy into what you are promoting.**

- ☐ **Questions make the other person feel important, and allow him or her to identify, clarify and express individual wants or needs.**

- ☐ **Questions involve the other person in the overall process.**

So, if questions are so vital, how do you ask the right ones? Here are eight principles for becoming a team-building Matlock:

(1) Prepare in advance the questions you will ask.

In virtually every area of business—whether you are a business owner, in upper management, on the frontline or in sales--there are several great opening questions you can ask. If you don't know which ones are best for you, ask a mentor or co-worker what works for them. One caution: Don't word questions in away that sounds canned or mechanical.

(2) Ask open-ended questions.

Closed questions that call for a "yes" or "no" answer tend to discourage people from talking, to give only limited information, and to set a negative tone. Open-ended questions help others tell you how they feel, what they want, or what they think.

(3) Ask need-questions.

You want to do more than get the other person to talk; you want him or her to talk about needs and wants. Frame questions that will give you insight into the way that person perceives his or her needs. Usually one major, overriding need comes to the surface when you ask the right question.

(4)   Avoid offensive questions or asking questions in an insensitive way.

Most of us have been "set-up" with questions since we were children. Parents asked, "What were you thinking when you…?" Teachers asked, "What did you do?" Most of us, as kids, learned quickly that no matter what answer we gave to some of these questions, we were going to "get it" anyway. So, be careful that you don't treat other adults the same way. Some examples of pitfalls to avoid are "set-up," nosey or intimidating inquiries. Don't condescend with your questions, whatever you do.

(5)   Start with broad queries, then move toward more narrow questions.

Broad inquiries are usually less threatening and produce more general information. They can help you get things rolling and steer you in the right direction. However, as your probing becomes more comfortable and picks up speed, you will need to get more specific with your questions.

(6)   Ask questions that are easy to answer.

None of us enjoys the "deer-in-front-of-the-headlights" feeling that happens when we blank out. Questions that require technical or specific knowledge can make the other person feel stupid. The savvier you make the other person feel, the better he or she will respond to you.

HAL GOOCH ♦ *STREET SMARTS* ♦ Proverb 10 ♦ 8

(7)   **Use questions to keep things moving positively.**

By skillfully using questions you can keep the conversation focused and moving in the right direction. Ask questions that people can easily respond to in a positive manner. If people ramble, questions can bring them back to the main areas of discussion. Studies have shown that most people much prefer to agree than to assert themselves and disagree. Make it easy to react positively

(8)   **Ask--then be quiet and listen.**

The other person cannot give you information as long as you keep talking. I've observed through the years that the best team-builders do 80% of the listening and 20% of the talking. The difference can be astounding in terms of your business-building success!

Questions are your greatest team-building tool. The better you become at asking questions, the easier it will be for you to achieve your goals as a businessperson. People who are demanding and confrontational close people up. Askers, though, often get what they want because people are more open to them.

LISTENING

Asking questions is vital, but **listening to the answers** is even more important. You must find a way to focus on the other person's needs, goals and dreams. To do that, you must become a masterful listener.

How do you develop and expand your listening skills? My suggestion is to practice and internalize these seven guidelines:

(1) Consciously reduce your talking time.

I've mentioned this before. You must understand that no matter who you are or the extent of your experience, you can easily talk too much. The first step to listening success is to accept that fact. During the next three or four business conversations, try to time how much you listen, as opposed to how much your prospect listens. See what your ratio is. You must know where you are before you can target any improvement. Don't expect perfection overnight. Learning is always full of relapses. Repeat this self-discipline every few weeks at first, then every month or two after you become adept at listening.

(2) Learn to ask discovery questions.

It may seem strange that listening requires good questioning skills, but to be a good listener, you must learn to ask those questions that will uncover the prospect's wants, needs and desires. Use these discovery phrases and questions:

"Tell me more . . ."

"How do you mean . . . ?"

"How will you . . . ?"

"If you were in my shoes, what would you . . . ?

"What do you think about . . . ?"

"How can I find out about . . . ?"

These lead-in questions and phrases will cause the other person to become involved and to explain.

(3) **When the other person speaks, listen.**

Does that sound simplistic? It is amazing to me how many people continue to speak when the other person attempts to talk. I have witnessed people who even increase their volume and speed of talking in order to override the other person and complete their thoughts. Maybe it is true that on the playground or among buddies, the battles are won by seeing who can out-shout and out-talk the opponent, but in real life and especially in team-building, the listener is always the winner.

(4) **As you listen, watch body language.**

Research shows more than 50% of communication is nonverbal. Some researchers up that figure to 90%. Watch especially for these:

- Good eye contact;
- A smile or other positive facial expressions;
- Either very relaxed posture or leaning forward; and,
- Complete attention.

If you are getting these body language signals, good for you. Press on. However, if you are seeing signals of discomfort or disagreement, you must change your approach and reset the stage. If the nonverbal communication is extremely negative or withdrawn, you may find that the only way out is to get back with the other person on another day.

(5) **Question what you hear.**

It is easy to rush to a conclusion without hearing out what the other person is really saying or wants to say. By reacting too quickly to questions, you can actually destroy the rapport and credibility you have built. Assume nothing. Listen carefully to the other person's complete comment or question before you answer.

Good listening requires practice. Put in the effort to listen and your team-building success will soar. By listening, you will position yourself as more knowledgeable and having greater expertise, and what could be better than that?

If all you want to talk about is yourself--your interests, your dreams, your products, your organization--you will undoubtedly encounter strong resistance and communication barriers. But if you focus your attention upon the other person's interests, needs, dreams, desires and values, you will notice a remarkable difference in that person's openness to you.

HAL GOOCH ♦ *STREET SMARTS* ♦ Proverb 10 ♦ 12

MATLOCK LIVES!

The better you become at asking questions and actively listening, the more often you can accomplish mutually-satisfying objectives with others as you build your team. This "Matlock" approach to probing separates the high achievers from those left wondering why they don't succeed. Remember Zig Ziglar's classic statement: "You can get everything you want out of life if you help enough other people get what they want."

The only way you can help others get what they want is to discover and uncover what is important to them. Do that by asking questions. Then be like the wise old owl and listen your way to success!

Proverb 11
"What gets rewarded gets done."

*"The desire to be appreciated is one of
the deepest drives in human nature.
If people want praise,
give them plenty of it."*

WILLIAM JAMES
Father of Modern Psychology

BUILDING VALUE IN YOUR TEAM

There are numerous traits that are recognized as ideal leadership qualities: loyalty, optimism, courage, decisiveness, tact, consideration, fairness, honesty, consistency and self-confidence. Regardless of your style or natural characteristics, however, you can become a great team- and dream-builder.

Whether you are a soft-spoken leader working with a curious mix of renegades and go-getters, or if you are an electrifying person who is forced to put up with security-seekers, I offer the following guidelines for boosting effective teamwork:

MOTIVATING OTHERS

`To be a success at teamwork, leverage and life, you must become proficient at motivating people, getting people to help accomplish mutually satisfying goals.

Do you want your children to behave? Do you want a better marriage? Do you need your co-workers to be more productive? Would you like others to notice and want to be part of your success? If so, Here are five ways you can motivate others positively:

(1)   Give others what they want FIRST.
People will generally work harder for emotional benefits and recognition than they will for monetary income. Think about it--through the years, young people have been willing to endure summer heat and laps around the gym for the

privilege of wearing a varsity uniform. Men and women have sacrificed everything for freedom and the flag. People are naturally drawn to be part of something worthwhile and exciting. Recognize this basic internal need, and you will tap into a supernatural team-building power.

(2) **Make people feel important.**
Human resource professionals insist that as much as 90% of the things we do in life are fueled by a desire to feel important. Seek genuine ways to be a team and individual cheerleader.

(3) **Offer positive feedback.**
The human psyche seems to move and feed on praise, affirmation and attention. People, in fact, will do more for recognition than for any other reward or payment. You can build this powerful drive by encouraging people to become better and do more.

(4) **Do simple favors for others.**
The Harvard Business School conducted an extensive test to determine how successful people earn the respect and cooperation of their co-workers. They found that one of the most effective techniques--developing a knack for doing simple favors--was also the easiest and least costly.

(5) Learn and use names.

The sweetest sound to a person in all the world is his or her name. We recognized this sound as infants, it has been reinforced through childhood and we are still enjoying it. No matter how old or grumpy we get, we still like for people to use our names. People have powerful feelings for a person who makes the extra effort to remember and use names.

(6) Be aware of people and value them.

Establish an atmosphere that will lead to satisfaction and desire in your team. Look people in the eye when you meet them. Focus on them and not the next person in the room. They should be the most important person in the world for those few seconds you are together.

(7) Be a great listener.

Proverb 10 was dedicated to this subject, but it is important enough to mention again in this discussion of recognition. It is not enough to ask questions. You must listen your way to teamwork success. Every person is more knowledgeable than you on certain subjects, and you can benefit from any employee or colleague as you consciously and openly learn from him or her.

(8) Encourage communication and approachability.

No matter how many or how few team-members or employees you have, encourage two-way movement through your door. Be inviting to employees who come to your office, but also practice management by walking around (MBWA).

(9) Be kind and forgiving toward others.

This seems so easy and simply, but look around at how many people you know who have forgotten how patient and gracious their mentors were? Realize that building great team-members and employees takes time. Nobody gets from kindergarten to graduate school in one step, and that principle is true in every area of life.

(10) Allow people to work through their own challenges.

Let them grow. Empowerment comes through a positive, people-building environment. You cannot keep every team-member or employee from making mistakes, nor should you. Give them the chance to learn by doing.

For one reason or another, too many leaders still handle all the big jobs and all the important work themselves. Or, when they do hand over a big assignment, they hover over the trainee or novice. Even if the job gets done, in the end, neither the leader nor the team-member gains very much.

HAL GOOCH ♦ STREET SMARTS ♦ Proverb 11 ♦ 6

(11) **Surprise people.**

Everybody expects a paycheck for work done, but who wouldn't enjoy a handwritten letter with a bonus for extra effort? The best leaders build teams by looking for ways to surprise their people. Gifts, cards, phone calls, impromptu picnics, notes, trips—these are just a few of the many ways you can surprise team-members.

Says Renn Zaphiropoulos, president of the Versatec Corporation: "When you give someone a check, don't mail it, have a celebration."

When you look for ways to surprise people there is a double payoff. The person feels great when you empower and value him or her through surprises, and you feel even better at making another person's day brighter.

(12) **Pass the pride along.**

Empower people. Recognize them. Show prompt appreciation for good ideas and good performance. Reward their creativeness and persistence. Your efforts to pass the pride along will be returned over and over again as your team grows.

The sum of your team will always be greater than its individual parts. A secret to your success is to develop your team's cohesiveness. After all, each of us is still a child, hardened a bit around the edges. We never really grow out of that constant need for praise and appreciation. If you understand these simple principles, you will be head-and-shoulders above others who want to attract and motivate a team of achievers.

REWARDS

If you want to have a profound impact in the game of life, develop the ability to believe in others and reward them. If you do, people will return your gift a thousand times.

In the future, successful leaders will be the most innovative leaders. They will promote teamwork throughout the organization. There be fewer and fewer places for whiners and prima-donnas on the team—among leaders, mid-managers or frontliners. It is an amazing thing when people are willing to work with each other in ways that reward the individual while profiting the entire team.

It's against the law, of course, to manufacture your own money, but nothing can stop you from manufacturing your own rewards and recognition. You can capitalize your growing business simply by being thoughtful and learning what encourages and motivates others. Forging a shared purpose and vision doesn't come easy or cheaply, as Epictetus noted almost 2000 years ago: "No great thing is created suddenly any more than is a bunch of grapes or a fig. If you tell me that you desire a fig, I answer you that there must be time. Let it first blossom, then become fruit, then ripen."

HAL GOOCH ♦ *STREET SMARTS* ♦ Proverb 11 ♦ 8

Your harvest can be a life changing experience when you learn and apply this proverb: What gets rewarded gets done!

Proverb 12
"Trust is the coin of the realm."

*"Example is not the main thing
in influencing others,
it is the only thing."*

--ALBERT SCHWEITZER

TRUST

I have spent most of my adult lifetime studying what makes people tick, especially high achievers. There aren't a lot of common characteristics among the most successful people in the world. Some are tall, some short. Some are handsome and beautiful, but others aren't. Some flaunt their successes, but most live relatively unspectacular lives. A lot enjoy wealth, but others live very simply. Many are great with people, but others are rude or boorish. Some are great communicators, while others, like me, are shy and even awkward.

However, virtually every person who is able to achieve and sustain great success in life is a great team-builder. The secret to great team-building can often be reduced to one word: TRUST.

So if you want to achieve much, build powerful teams. To do that, build trust. To build trust, you must develop these three trust-builders: HONESTY, INTEGRITY and COURAGE. Let's focus on each one.

HONESTY

Virtually every major survey of desirable leadership characteristics places one characteristic at the top of the list: HONESTY. What is it? According to Webster's Dictionary, it means to be held in respect, to be free from deceit.

HAL GOOCH ♦ *STREET SMARTS* ♦ Proverb 12 ♦ 3

The American Management Association recently surveyed thousands of workers, asking them what they considered to be the most important leadership traits. The majority, 83% to be exact, expressed belief that a person must be honest before workers are willing to grant that individual the title "leader."

That's what workers say about their superiors. What do leaders say about workers? Learning Systems of Stamford, Connecticut, polled a number of the nation's leading senior executives, asking them to identify and rank the personal qualities they hope to find in their employees. Honesty ranked first on the list. Loyalty was a close second.

Yet according to a *New York Times/* CBS poll, only 32% of those in the workplace believe that fellow-workers are truly honest. There is clearly a gap between what we admire and we think we are getting.

You can do it right. As a STREET SMART achiever, you must project honesty. These means confrontation when necessary, a painful process that all of us avoid. Positive things will never happen until people trust you, and it all begins with honesty.

The rewards for being honest are immeasurable, not just the immediate benefits, but in terms of sustained leadership and long-range productivity. And remember, honesty isn't measured by degrees. You either have it or you don't!

INTEGRITY

Henry Clay, a great American statesman of the nineteenth century, planned to introduce a certain bill in Congress. A friend expressed alarm: "If you do, Clay, it will kill your chance for the presidency."

"But is the measure right?" Clay asked.

When his friend assured the statesman it was correct, Clay is recorded as announcing, "Then I would rather be right than president."

Integrity!

This trait, which is defined as having sound moral principle, goes beyond honesty. Honesty suggests being free of deceit. Integrity suggests doing what is right, no matter what. Doing right and being consistent in what you say and what you do is one of the greatest tests in life. It is also an absolute necessity if you want to build a strong business that will stand the tests of time.

COURAGE

In an age of corporate raiding, fast-tracking and back-stabbing, being a "stand-up," courageous person is not easy, and it's seldom popular.

HAL GOOCH ♦ *STREET SMARTS* ♦ Proverb 12 ♦ 5

What is courage? A basic definition is "the attitude of facing and dealing with anything recognized as dangerous, difficult or painful." More to the point, courage measures your achievement abilities at critical times in life, and it can only be developed in the stress and strain of everyday activities.

- ☐ Courage means keeping your word, no matter what.
- ☐ Courage often involves impacting others positively.
- ☐ Courage forces you to recognize and admit personal mistakes and to learn from those failures.
- ☐ Courage sometimes includes standing alone, despite the personal or professional costs.

Undoubtedly, you can add many other specifics to my list. Here's the bottom line, without courage, you will never be a great, lasting success. History has proved that fact again and again.

Courage often requires holding on five minutes or a day or a week longer, even when everyone around you is telling you to quit. It means seeing what is right, and then doing it.

Of all the leaders in the world who have lived during my lifetime, I believe the greatest example of courage was President Ronald Reagan. He stood against totalitarian aggressors, dared to push for less government bureaucracy and outwitted the liberal media by taking his ideas directly to the American people. After the assassination attempt, when he lingered near death, he joked and reassured both the doctors and public. He encouraged us to rebuild a demoralized military. He helped people of all generations believe in America and patriotism again. He did it with few supporters in Washington and even fewer in the media. Yet during his presidency we witnessed the weakening of Communism, the cracking of the Iron Curtain, the strengthening of freedom around the world and the foundation for unprecedented economic recovery. That's courage in my book!

DEPTH

The only way you can build a great team is through trust. The only way you can build trust is through honesty, integrity and courage. How do you rate yourself in these areas? More importantly, are you willing to improve any area where you need to strengthen?

Trust is vital. Remember the oft-quoted words from Edward R. Murrow, one of the world's most-loved journalists and news commentators: "To be persuasive we must be believable; to be believable we must be credible; to be credible, we must be truthful."

Trust is one of the hardest attributes to earn. It is also one of the most fragile to sustain. It is earned minute by minute, hour by hour, month by month, year by year. Sadly, it can also be lost quickly. People are willing to forgive a few minor transgressions, a slip of the tongue, a misspoken word, a careless act, but there comes a time when enough is enough. And whether you are an elected leader, a team-builder, a manager or a parent, when you have used up all your earned trust, you will find that it is nearly impossible to earn it back.

That's why Thomas Watson, then CEO of IBM, often shared his feelings on the subject: "I firmly believe that any corporation, in order to survive and achieve success, must have a sound set of beliefs. Next, I believe that the most important factor in corporate success is faithful adherence to those beliefs."

In every area of your life, you will prosper best when you are honest, filled with integrity and courageous. Upon these three foundations, you can be trusted to build a powerful team and a profitable business.

Proverb 13
"Don't talk the talk without walking the walk."

"What you are speaks so loudly that I cannot hear what you say."

--RALPH WALDO EMERSON
Nineteenth Century Poet

HAL GOOCH ♦ *STREET SMARTS* ♦ Proverb 13 ♦ 2

LASTING EXAMPLES

I read a classic essay many years ago that made a lasting impression. It still bears reading:

When Johnny was 6 years old, he was with his father when they were caught speeding. His father handed the officer a twenty-dollar bill with his driver's license. "It's OK, son," his father said as they drove off. "Everybody does it."

When he was 8, he was present at a family council presided over by Uncle George, on the surest means to shave points off the income tax return. "It's OK, kid," his uncle said. "Everybody does it."

When he was 9, his mother took him to his first theater production. The box office man couldn't find any seats until his mother discovered an extra $5 in her purse. "It's OK, son," she said. "Everybody does it.'

When he was 12, he broke his glasses on the way to school. His Aunt Francine persuaded the insurance company that they had been stolen and they collected $75. "It's OK, kid," she said. "Everybody does it."

HAL GOOCH ♦ STREET SMARTS ♦ Proverb 13 ♦ 3

When he was 15, he made right guard on the high school football team. His coach showed him how to block and at the same time grab the opposing end by the shirt so the official couldn't see it. "It's OK, kid," the coach said. "Everybody does it."

When he was 16, he took his first summer job at the supermarket. His assignment was to put the overripe strawberries in the bottom of the boxes and the good ones on top where they would show. "It's OK, kid," the manager said. "Everybody does it."

"When he was 18, Johnny and a neighbor applied for a college scholarship. Johnny was a marginal student. His neighbor was in the upper three percent of his class, but he couldn't play right guard. Johnny got the scholarship. "It's OK, son," his parents said. "Everybody does it."

When he was 19, he was approached by an upperclassman who offered the test answers for $50. "It's OK, kid," he said. "Everybody does it."

Johnny was caught and sent home in disgrace. "How could you do this to your mother and me?'" His father said. "You never learned anything like this at home." His aunt and uncle were also shocked.

HAL GOOCH ♦ *STREET SMARTS* ♦ Proverb 13 ♦ 4

If there's one thing the adult world can't stand, it's a kid who cheats!

What does a story like that have to do with STREET SMARTS and business and success? Everything! The way you see yourself determines how you will be viewed and treated by every person you meet. Only you can understand your purpose in life and then build upon that foundation to believe in yourself and attract others who believe in you. So it is up to you to make a deep commitment to excellence, to accepting nothing less than your best.

As part of learning how to "walk the walk," instead of merely "talk the talk," let me give you ten practical guidelines to motivate yourself to be a STREET SMART success every day:

(1)   Be extra proficient.

Do your homework better than anyone else. If you want to be recognized as a professional, then be professional! Develop a keen insight into the attitudes of the people on the team you are building. In other words, never stop learning.

(2)   Be more credible than others.

To be successful, you must persuade. To persuade, you must educate. To educate, you must be believable and trustworthy. Believability is a strength which is born through experience and strength of character.

(3) Be more flexible.

Most of us tend to get set in our ways. The best in any field of endeavor, however, keep looking for a way to do something better. Don't change merely for change's sake, but develop a willingness to change. Learn to recognize new advances and innovations; this will keep you ahead of the pack.

(4) Be extra consistent.

Just because you are currently doing well in your profession or business doesn't mean that you are successful. Instead, judge your success based upon this question: "Am I consistently doing the very best I can with the skills and talents I have?" Consistency is one of the most important character traits needed by any sales professional who seeks to rise above the rest.

(5) Be extra honest.

As mentioned in previous proverbs, people should be able to count on you, to depend on and believe in you. In virtually every corporate and marketplace survey of desired characteristics, integrity is the highest-rated. To achieve long-term success in any business, you have to be honest and possess a record of living up to your commitments.

(6) Be more well-groomed and mannered than others.

We haven't discussed appearances in STREET SMARTS to this point, but it's common sense that people want to be around others who are neat in appearance, dress, hygiene and demeanor.

While we are spotlighting the subject of "walking the walk," you should get in as good of physical condition as possible and stay that way. Your automobile should be the cleanest in the parking lot. Your clothes, whether they are from Brooks Brothers or Sears, should always be clean, pressed and well coordinated. It's simply a matter of personal pride.

(7) Be extra resilient.

Building a business is not always an easy road. In fact, I can tell you without any reservations that you will discover what you have inside sooner, rather than later. Still, you must persevere. This is such an important subject that Proverb 20 deals exclusively with persistence. You will not succeed without it.

(8) Be more organized and time-conscious than others.

Time is a natural resource which, when spent, will never return. Furthermore, the success you enjoy tomorrow will be in direct proportion to your ability to manage time today.

HAL GOOCH ♦ STREET SMARTS ♦ Proverb 13 ♦ 7

You must understand the importance of doing weekly planners--listing the activities that you must accomplish in the week, then breaking those down into daily and hourly activities. Success, in fact, hinges on your ability to maximize your time!

Do you keep "To Do" lists? Does your desk, calendar, notebook and automobile reflect the kind of person with whom you would like to do business? Don't always be ruled by the urgent and immediate. Don't let poor planning cause an endless series of "emergencies." Focus on the most important priorities, and develop a system for getting your life in order. The daily effort to "walk the walk" will pay off handsomely.

(9) **Stand out from the crowd.**

Ordinary people do things in ordinary ways. Extraordinary people do things in extraordinary ways. Develop your own style. Be memorable. Whether you are making a business presentation or team-building, use your talents and blend them with a little bit of showbiz.

I am not encouraging you to be tacky or eccentric, but I do know that the best businesspeople have a talent for making an impact on the opinions and actions of others--an influence so subtle that it may go unrecognized at first.

(10) Be extra enthusiastic.

The final four letters of the word "enthusIASM" explain everything:

I

Am

Sold

Myself

Sell yourself first--on your purpose in life, your family, your country, your organization and your products. Once you are sold, you will have no trouble being enthusiastic about promoting your team-building ideals.

The top professionals in any field have an ability to make things happen. Why? It often revolves around one word--enthusiasm!

How do you rate in each of these 10 areas? Determine your weak points, then develop a plan of action and write specific goals as to how you are going to improve those characteristics.

SET AN EXAMPLE

A leader leads. By actually pounding nails, former President Jimmy Carter did more to promote the Habitat for Humanity than by any persuasive speech or television public service announcement he could have made. Suddenly Habitat volunteers began showing up in droves to help build homes for deserving low-income families all over the nation.

Why? A leader leads.

Walking the walk is immeasurably more important than talking the talk. Your children and colleagues will remember what you do, and they will follow your example, not your words.

Now it is up to you to walk your powerful walk, one step at a time!

Proverb 14
"Take care of the little guy and he'll take care of you."

"There are no such things as service industries. There are only industries whose service components are greater or less than those of other industries. Everybody is in service."

DR. THEODORE LEVITT
Harvard Business School Professor

HAL GOOCH ♦ STREET SMARTS ♦ Proverb 14 ♦ 2

CUSTOMERS

I'm sure than many businesspeople have yellowed copies of this superb article that was written years ago under t he title, "The Name Means the Same:"

The lawyer calls him a client.

The doctor calls him a patient.

The hotel calls him a guest.

The editor calls him a subscriber.

The broadcaster calls him a listener-viewer.

The cooperative calls him a patron.

The retailer calls him a shopper.

The educator calls him a student.

The manufacturer calls him a dealer.

The politician calls him a constituent.

The banker calls him a depositor-borrower.

The minister calls him a parishioner.

You may give a professional name to the person who buys your product or service, but no matter what you call him, he is always the customer.

HAL GOOCH ♦ *STREET SMARTS* ♦ Proverb 14 ♦ 3

Thankfully, before my wife Susan and I began our own marketing and consulting business in 1972, we had already learned the importance of "taking care of the little guy," as some people call it. I was in the furniture manufacturing business, so the ultimate customer was clearly the person who bought what we made. Susan was a nine-to-five computer operator, so she was comfortable in dealing with the public. As we began developing what would eventually become a worldwide business, we both realized, however, how much we had to learn as we discovered an entirely new set of customers.

You see, no matter who you are or what you do, you and your team have "customers" whom you must serve better than your competition does. Arrogance is business suicide. Without satisfied and loyal customers—by whatever name you call them—you simply won't succeed in business.

CUSTOMER SERVICE BASICS

Everybody talks about customer service. Wherever you go, you see posters and plaques pointing to the importance of keeping customers happy. In truth, though, we live in an age where understanding and application of even basic customer care will put you head-and-shoulders above nearly everyone else.

Here is your challenge: In an age of carelessness and shoddy work, can you go the "extra mile" and do the things no one else seems willing to do? More importantly, as you develop your team, can you impact others to have the same "customer-is-royalty" attitude?

Sometimes people around my hometown jokingly refer to a nearby North Carolina town as "LA." Susan and I actually lived in "LA." In our case, though, it stands for Lower Archdale, not Los Angeles. But whether you live in North Carolina's LA or California's LA or anywhere in the world, you must realize that you have to be concerned with becoming a customer service master, not just because it is the "in" thing to do, but because it is the right thing to do. The unique person who decides to do whatever it takes to deliver value-added service becomes a member of a select group.

Regardless if you are a one-person startup enterprise doing business with a cell phone and tons of energy, or even if you are the CEO of a large corporation—you can make a difference by shifting more and more toward top-quality customer service. Here are the basic ways to begin:

(1) Empower your team.

As mentioned previously, whether you can assemble your team in a telephone booth or even if you can already fill the Georgia Dome with your associates, a great customer service attitude must be a conscious decision throughout the organization.

For starters, it's not really true that the customer should be first. Your team members are first. How you treat your team will be reflected in the way they treat other team members. How you treat your team will be magnified in the way the team treats your customers. There's no way to instill a positive customer service mentality unless you first live and give this vital concept throughout your organization. Build your team first, and you form the foundation for a strong organization. Upon that foundation you must forge a widespread focus on customer care.

(2) **Understand that you are in the PEOPLE BUSINESS, first and foremost.**

Whether you are a secretary, salesperson, share-cropper or surgeon, you must "sell" your products or services to people. The most difficult thing to find is well-motivated, highly trained and concerned achievers who are willing and able to offer great customer care. When you do provide "second mile" service, you stand out like a beautiful rose in the midst of winter.

Think of your life during the past few weeks--how many times do you remember when anyone in the marketplace treated you as if you were royalty? Okay, how many times did the businesses even acknowledge that you were alive? Enough said!

(3) **Focus on your customer, whomever he or she may be.**

Is this idea old-fashioned and obsolete, or what? Hardly! It is your future, if you want to be in business very long. Don't just talk about customer service. Do it. A quality service program will fail, but a quality service consciousness will succeed. The difference is staggering.

If you are a salesperson, for example, get beyond giving out imprinted pens, college football tickets, glad-handing and "How-ya-doing?" remarks, and seek deeply into a client's real wants. Focus on your customer's needs, desires and problems.

(4) **Understand who your competition is and then out serve them.**

Just as everyone has customers, regardless of what you call them, you also have competitors if you are in any business. You must first know who your competition is. Then you must understand your competition before you can expect to discover solutions.

Service is the key to your business. Relationships are important. In fact, whatever you do, in terms of customer care, will make you stand out from the competition. Service, in general, is so negative that the smallest things you do to make customers feel special are powerfully positive.

Out-serving the competition can require lots of creativity and effort. For example, internet services—email or web sites—or financial services--credit cards, mortgages or online banking—are all marketplaces of similar services. With minor differences, everyone is essentially "selling" the same thing. This is when great customer care becomes THE critical issue.

(5) Push decisions as close as possible to the customer.

This should be obvious, but it is also very rare. How many times have you stood in line while the gum-smacking grocery store cashier pages and re-pages a manager to come to the front to make a decision about a fifty-cent pack of whatever? Or how often have you sat on hold, listening to "Feelings" for the thirteenth time, while a CSR (Customer Service Representative) tries to track down a CSM (Customer Service Manager)?

Empowering your people means educating them, then letting them make decisions (within reason, of course). Team-members in a customer-friendly organization must become very good at making decisions.

(6) Recognize your customers personally in meaningful, creative ways.

Try recognizing customers personally (and this would certainly include your team-members who are your most important customers) personally. This can include such simple things as birthday cards or thank you notes.

In Greensboro, not far from my North Carolina home, every team-member on a leading orthodontist's staff is trained to write at least three "thinking-of-you" notes to patients. Even the doctor does this, and you can only imagine how the "word of mouth" benefits have spread throughout the area.

HAL GOOCH ♦ *STREET SMARTS* ♦ Proverb 14 ♦ 8

You probably have your own favorite stories of the waitress who remembers the way you like your breakfast or the mechanic who treats your car with extra respect. You don't forget these special touches.

No matter what your business is or what you call your customers, your thoughtfulness will pay off financially, and you will feel good doing something that others would never think of doing!

(7) **Ask for continual feedback from your mentors, teammates and customers.**

You must ASK and SEEK for this information. No news is not always good news. Of course, no one knows everything about the needs and desires of your customers. And if you think you do know everything, you will undoubtedly be left in marketplace dust. After all, disgruntled customers often fade into the sunset, using word-of-mouth advertising to take lots of other potential customers with them.

Seek feedback from everywhere you can get it. Leaving a few "how-are-we-doing?" survey forms on restaurant tables, for example, will probably leave the café owners with an incomplete snapshot of customer satisfaction. The owner might be better served by spending time with both customers and waitresses.

In fact, if you are a business owner or in management, one of the best places to glean important information is always by talking with frontline employees—the receptionist, the salesperson, the front-desk person. But even that is only a partial picture. That's why the best customer care corporations spend huge amounts of time and money seeking to peer inside past, present and future customers.

It is crucial that you know your customer. Nothing in the world can replace sound knowledge of his or her wants, needs and complaints.

(8) **Always be learning.**

The marketplace is constantly changing. Your workplace is unceasingly shifting. You must learn how to provide quality service to your customers--not 75% or 80% of the time--but as close to 100% of the time as possible.

How can you make your business more customer-friendly? Can you improve your telephone skills or build a more accessible website? If you have a store or office, does your reception or walk-in area reek with unfriendliness and barriers, or is it warm and hospitable?

(9) **Keep your word.**

This is the final guideline, but it is one of the most important. Never break your promises, whatever the cost. One failure raises doubt, the next one raises tempers. More judgement errors invite others to talk about you behind your back.

Repeated failures will inevitably damage your reputation. Make fewer promises and only make promises that you absolutely, positively intend to fulfill.

Without a strong, team-wide, values-based commitment to customer service, you quite probably will not survive the increasingly turbulent marketplace.

CARE

A quick glance around any area of the marketplace provides living proof that there are few individuals or companies putting forth the kind of extra-mile effort required to provide great customer care. That knowledge, if you are willing to act upon it, can add up to a virtual gold mine for you!

Ask, "What is the real purpose of our business?" The answer, no matter how you ask it, is **customers**. And no matter where you work in the marketplace—entrepreneur, CEO, front-liner, mid-management--you are a salesperson and customer service representative. The better job you do in the people business, the greater your chances for long-term success.

As marketplace pressure grows more intense, customer satisfaction will make the difference in helping you thrive, both now and in the future. In fact, great customer care is already the business of businesses.

Proverb 15
"Culture keeps what enthusiasm gets."

"Enthusiasm is one of the most powerful engines of success. When you do a thing, do it with all your might. Put your whole soul into it. Stamp it with your own personality. Be active, be energetic, be enthusiastic and faithful, and you will accomplish your object. Nothing great was ever achieved without enthusiasm."

RALPH WALDO EMERSON

TEAM SPIRIT

Whether you're running a sports franchise, a hamburger joint, a distribution network or A multi-billion dollar internet company, you must foster and develop a deep loyalty to your team. Logos on hats, T-shirts, ballpoint pens and office banners are merely outward tokens. What happens inside the team to ignite and sustain spirit is one of the most important elements you can foster.

How do you create an enthusiastic corporate culture?

Knowing what to do is important, of course. Knowing what NOT to do to ignite a powerful *esprit de corps* is also vital, especially as you lead people.

WHY TEAMS FAIL

There are many unknowns which can cause organizational disaster: bad economy, overwhelming competition, right time/wrong place, takeovers, governmental intervention and more. More often, failure is leader-related, rather than some external force. You may be able to add other ideas from your own experience, but here are a several that I've seen—the main reasons why teams fail:

HAL GOOCH ♦ *STREET SMARTS* ♦ Proverb 15 ♦ 3

☐ **When leaders don't motivate well**

Low motivation is almost always a problem that leads to failure. Unfortunately, when energy and productivity are down, the typical leader or manager will deal with it by attempting to motivate his or her people through slogans and rah-rah speeches rather than getting to such core issues as values, purpose, vision and alignment. Motivational talks and programs can increase the energy level and short-term success, but unless some substance is involved, motivational methods become little more than a candy bar-type panaceas. When the sugar hits the system, it may increase the energy level for a short while, but quickly the energy level will undoubtedly plummet as the sugar burns out.

I believe in motivation, properly used. Increasing the energy level of a company is useful. The question is this: What are you motivating people toward? That is the question that often goes unanswered in the dizzying excitement of typical motivational moments.

☐ **When leaders don't paint the big picture**

For long-term success, people have a definite need to feel part of something bigger than themselves. I have met few people, if any, who honestly enjoy merely working as an unimportant cog in a large corporate or organizational machine. Becoming part of the big picture and participating in the achievement of shared values is extremely important.

Is it any wonder that such people fail or resign themselves to mediocrity when they don't feel important to the process?

☐ **When people are not educated or trained sufficiently**

People often fail, quite simply, because they are expected to do things for which they have never been prepared. Leaders tend to take resumes seriously and team-members often cover up inadequacies. The education and training of each team-member is one function that cannot be avoided or relegated to occasional group sessions. Whether you are preparing someone for a company promotion or to achieve higher levels in your organization, there is no substitute for one-on-one training. Get people to read books, listen to tapes, attend seminars, learn from mentors—there are an unlimited number of ways to educate. When people understand how to do something, the success level almost always rises dramatically.

☐ **When leaders are afraid of failure**

Leaders may fail simply because they don't understand the value of occasionally failing. They may be limited by their inability to put themselves on the line. They may have great ideas but lack the courage or conviction to sell those ideas to others. Such so-called leaders try to prevent a fall by avoiding action; in doing so actually accelerate their own ruin.

HAL GOOCH ♦ *STREET SMARTS* ♦ Proverb 15 ♦ 5

How you handle failures and disappointments can often be the thing that makes or breaks your leadership climb. If you learn from your mistakes, your leadership breakdowns may prove to be your greatest assets.

- **When leaders lack the ability or willingness to support others**

Not nearly enough leaders of corporations or organizations foster support. Too often, everyone is more or less told to watch their own backsides and never get too supportive of anyone else.

These problems will not go away. The biggest challenge is that not enough companies have leaders who have the enthusiasm and endurance required to overcome these common failures. STREET SMARTS leaders can work to overcome their own failures while seeking to help team-members face their challenges. That is the essence of teamwork and leadership. And the principles of fostering strong team spirit are quite simple to learn and teach.

ENTHUSIASTIC LEADERSHIP

Conventional thinking, based on the boss/hired-hand mindset, tends to stifle initiative, creativity, innovation and teamwork. A values-based environment, however, energizes and promotes everyone within the organization. How?

HAL GOOCH ♦ *STREET SMARTS* ♦ Proverb 15 ♦ 6

(1)   **Build ownership among the entire team.**

Ownership is a special condition created when people see their organization's purpose as an extension of their personal purposes. When employees emotionally and consciously "buy" into an organization's goals, they also assume responsibility for the company's success by embracing the vision as their own and by sharing accountability for achieving it.

(2)   **Network with others.**

Networking, in a corporate sense, means people talking to each other, sharing ideas, information and resources. It a time-honored process and is more more efficient than any other process.

Our high-tech world has created a great need for high-touch relationships. Any leader or business which ignores the desire for energized interaction is destined to fail.

(3)   **Ask, don't tell.**

The telling method implies control, indicates manipulation and triggers "bad blood" between authority figures and subordinates. When an asking mindset permeates a company, it encourages creativity, inspires participation and reduces resistance to change.

Japanese managers traditionally have asked every worker to add ideas. And Japanese experts--for instance, engineers--live on the factory floor, supporting the worker. American companies are learning. More than 900 companies, organizations and government agencies in the United States have structured programs for encouraging suggestions. During one year, those suggestions have saved their companies at least $2.2 billion. For those suggestions that were adopted, during the same year visionary companies paid $160 million in awards for suggestions that were adopted.

One program of a leading natural gas company encourages employees to generate innovative ideas and methods that help the utility to be competitive, increase revenue and reduce the cost of service. Employees are encouraged to submit as many ideas as possible. The ideas are evaluated by a number of experts. The person whose idea is judged "Best Idea of the Year" receives a hefty bonus which is presented at team meetings.

One of the greatest ways to foster a team spirit, in any organization, is establish an orientation toward asking, versus telling. By asking questions, you help people buy in. You give them value. This continual quest of asking people what they want and what they need, is one of the most effective mindsets for any company or organization that desires to survive and succeed in the years to come.

(4) Build interactive, open communication.

Traditional structures, including physical locations and middle management's desire to use information as a power tool, thwart good corporate communication flow. In the fast-paced, high-tech business world, these established patterns will be discarded in favor of flexible frameworks (primarily computerized and internet systems) which facilitate the quick flow of information.

(5) Foster innovation throughout the organization.

Companies are increasingly challenged to search for better procedures, merchandizing and services. Accelerated changes in the marketplace have created the absolute necessity for better innovation. STREET SMARTS leaders can never stop urging, "Let's find a better way to do this--together."

(6) Have fun with your team.

Sure, you have a job to do. Of course, you each have roles to play. But life is too short to see work as a series of mindless, thankless tasks. You have to find a way to make work interesting and, yes, even fun.

Few leaders have held more responsible, demanding positions than the late Harold Geneen, the man who turned a faltering ITT into a giant conglomerate dealing in everything from Wonder Bread to Avis cars (while sales skyrocketed from $766 million to $22 billion). In describing how he built such excellence in team spirit during his time as top leader of ITT from 1959 until 1977, Geneen told people: "I wanted to create an invigorating, challenging, creative atmosphere at ITT. I wanted to get the people there to reach for goals that they might think were beyond them. I wanted them to accomplish more than they thought was possible. And I wanted them to do it not only for the company and their careers, but also for the fun of it. I wanted them to enjoy the process of tackling a difficult piece of business, solving it, and going on to bigger, better, and tougher challenges. I wanted them to do this, not for self-aggrandizement, but as part of a greater team effort, in which each player realized his own contribution to the team, knew that he was needed and appreciated, and took pride and self-satisfaction from playing a winning game."

Lighten up! Everyone winds up a winner by sharing positive, team-spirit attitudes with others in a creative, fun atmosphere.

(7) **Be excited about change**

Change must be seen as beneficial, creating a win-win situation for everyone. One of the greatest challenges for today's leaders is to help employees who have become accustomed to functioning in large, impersonal, bureaucratic conglomerates, to understand the meaning of creative freedom.

Only when people buy into the organization's purpose and understand the meaning of their contributions to the organization's overall success, will change be seen as necessary and beneficial.

How can you succeed as a STREET SMARTS leader? Start by being increasingly aware of the necessity for true, enthusiastic teamwork. If ever corporations and organizations needed value-conscious, quality-minded, service-oriented, team-minded leaders, that time is now.

IGNITING TEAM SPIRIT

Leadership is getting a group of people to move in a direction toward a worthwhile goal. This team concept works well in athletics. Business is also beginning to see the importance of team spirit. It is critical for you, as a leader, to develop not only a teamwork mentality, but mental ownership of the overall vision and goals. The concept of teamwork and building a culture of enthusiasm for the organization is not a passing fad.

People can be united by email, a tape-of-the-week program, national or regional conventions, incentive programs, team meetings, televised get-togethers—all work well. Community is the key. Team spirit has ignited organizations to spread Microsoft, the Amway Corporation and Coca-Cola around the world. It has helped the Houston Comets (WNBA) and the glory teams of the Chicago Bulls (NBA) to forge championship dynasties. A passion for high achievement has built McDonalds and Wal-Mart into monumental institutions.

And it can happen when you foster ownership throughout the team! Build the fire, fuel the enthusiasm and watch it spread. The excitement that follows goes far beyond slogans and rah-rah sessions. This kind of excitement becomes a culture for the entire organization. When that happens, everyone is a winner!

Proverb 16
"Be willing to learn from the out-of-town expert with the briefcase."

    Few people succeed in any enterprise without mentors. It is vital to find someone who can help "teach you the ropes." Some mentors help in spite of themselves, but the best ones are remembered for caring and sharing the most important lessons in business and life."

HAL GOOCH ♦ *STREET SMARTS* ♦ **Proverb 16 ♦ 2**

THE VALUE OF MENTOR RELATIONSHIPS

Most people have heard the Bible verse, "A prophet is without honor in his own land." If you doubt its truth, wait until you have teenage children. Any parent can tell you war-stories of trying to instill certain principles over and over with seemingly little effect. Then, without warning, the young person comes puppeting the same principle, spoken by a teacher, a friend or a spiritual leader. Suddenly, because someone else affirmed what you've been trying to teach, the teenager finally gets it.

Okay, be honest. Doesn't it hurt a little bit that your teenager didn't "get it" when you were talking to him or her? The same thing happens over and over in the corporate world. Because of your close proximity to the people with whom you work everyday, you will seldom have the respect of the out-of-town expert. People almost always listen to someone who comes from the "outside." So what? You can fight against the "prophet without honor" principle, or you can use it to your advantage.

Begin by understanding the value of mentorships. You see, powerful people don't waste time and energy comparing themselves with others. Such comparisons can rob them of their power. If we're using energy being vain or bitter because people in your organization learn from out-of-town experts, then you are losing the opportunity to be productive and powerful. Instead, find mentors wherever you can, however you can. How?

Whether you are an entrepreneur or in a more rigid corporate setting, mentors can be found anywhere and everywhere. There are all kinds of mentors in life, and they all don't have to be career associated. Sometimes, we choose mentors to help us through personal challenges or to enhance our enjoyment of life. Mentors sometimes come into our lives in mysterious ways. Mine certainly have. There is an old Chinese proverb: "When the student is ready, the teacher appears." I have found that each time I was ready for the next challenge, a mentor came into my life. There have been a handful of people who have had a tremendous effect on my life, and I definitely consider them my mentors.

Of course, this doesn't mean we can simply wait for people or things to knock us over to signal their arrival. We must be open and receptive to the arrival of our mentors. Many times, it is much later, after we've viewed the relationship in retrospect, when we understand the reason for their appearance.

MENTOR PROGRAMS

No matter where you work, the evidence is overwhelming that people, not new buildings or advanced machines, are the driving force behind economic growth. Edward Dennison, the growth-economics expert who brought quality to new levels in America, believes that one-third of our gross national product increases of recent years was caused by the increase in the education level of our work force. Dennison also believes that at least half of the GNP growth was the result of technology innovation and increased know-how, which also depend on education. That leaves just 15% of the total increase as a result of more capital equipment and buildings. Though by no means an exhaustive list, here are several worthwhile educational processes that serve the purpose of empowering people:

☐ **Educational programs**

In a competitive and rapidly changing economy, old skills become outdated quickly and new skills are needed perpetually. Most of us will change occupations at least three times and jobs at least six times. Those statistics are bound to increase, perhaps double, during the next quarter-century. Today's leaders must help prepare employees for those changes?

☐ **In-service education**

Xerox, for example, has a campus-like education center at Leesburg, Virginia, from which it directs the activities of 97 training branches around the country. McDonald's has its "Hamburger U." The Amway Corporation is known around the world for its innovative leadership education programs. Domino's Pizza and the Milliken Company have also been in-service education pacesetters.

☐ **Self-development opportunities**

The best mentoring organization make books, cassettes and seminars available to everyone. If your organization has a tape-of-the-week program, take advantage of it. If you have educational or inspiration get-togethers which are available to you, be there, no matter what it takes.

- **College degree or advanced degree education**

    More organizations are supporting an employee's pursuit of job-related college degrees by paying (or reimbursing) full or partial tuition.

- **Adventure learning**

    More and more leaders are learning by doing unfamiliar and challenging physical or psychological activities. Steve McCormick, director of Colorado Outward Bound, and Larry Wilson, who heads the Pecos River Learning Center, are pacesetters in combining leadership education with survival, fitness and wilderness training.

- **Week-long or Weekend Retreats**

    Fewer organizations are endorsing executive golf and tennis get-aways, supposedly disguised as planning retreats. More and more corporations are moving toward "nuts and bolts" strategic sessions with wellness training breaks. One of the most effective components of individual education is to get an entire group to spend several days together in an intensive time of communication and activity. The results can be vital for the long-term, overall health of an organization.

Whether your organization or company has mentoring or leadership development programs or not, for you to succeed in the corporate environment, you have one of the oldest, strongest and least expensive forces already available to you--mentor relationships. The mentor relationship is a critical element in building effective careers.

HAL GOOCH ♦ *STREET SMARTS* ♦ Proverb 16 ♦ 6

MENTORS

The concept of seeking out a sponsor or mentor is hardly new. It has grown from a hardy history of apprenticeships typical of the craft trades and professions such as law and medicine. The original Mentor was the trusted counselor of Odysseus, and later of his son, Telemachus.

But mentoring, as viewed today, doesn't encompass formal roles as much as it does relationships. Even though mentoring relationship often flourish in work settings, they can also evolve informally. Friends, neighbors and relatives can all act as mentors if you are constantly seeking to learn from others.

Companies have researched the subject of mentoring during recent years. One common thread that runs throughout the research data is this: Mentoring is vital in career building. Mentors can help new managers learn important skills. Mentors can model ways to attack problems and develop solutions. A mentor offers specific examples of what to do in order to qualify for a particular position or for promotion. The mentor can help you build a better team. The emphasis is on skill and behavior. The role need not be professional in today's usage. Frequently the mentor demonstrates not only behavioral skills, but the underlying attitudes as well.

In education, the professor's most important role is to motivate the student to pursue continuing scholarship throughout his or her life, and to acquire a sound value system and the capacity for independent thought. The same could be said for corporate coaches and organizational mentors.

Here are a few guidelines that I have found invaluable for maximizing mentor relationship:

(1) **Realize that there are incredible opportunities all around you for mentoring relationships.**

   Every leader is seeking some form of immortality, and no form of immortality can be more rewarding or emotionally profitable than when a teacher reproduces himself or herself through a student. Keep your ears open. If you want to learn from leaders, seek to be in the midst of leaders.

(2) **Seek mentoring relationships honestly, not purely for promotion or prestige.**

   Mentorship implies relationship, and a relationship usually cannot exist purely for selfish gain. Mentorship is a two-way street.

(3) **Know your place in the mentoring relationship.**

   While mentors may be good teachers, most are unwilling to share power. Mentors may even run the risk of over-controlling. They can be like perfectionist parents who have a lot of knowledge and experience to share, but who want their children to be mirror images of themselves and to do things the way they have always done. You may have to walk a tightrope--you need to learn from politically seasoned and technically experienced mentors, but you desire freedom and responsibility as well. Somehow you must find a balance as you prepare for the future.

(4) **Listen actively to what your mentor says.**

How simple, you say! Sadly, my research shows that a startling number of mentor relationships fail simply because people do not strive aggressively to understand the mentor's point of view. Even if you don't like or agree with what you hear, you can still understand and learn.

(5) **Be sensitive to the mentor's comments and criticisms.**

Some leaders enjoy posing a confusing question just to force you to take a side on issues. Other mentors, however, have little place for proteges who argue with them. With this type of person, ask lots of questions and seek to clarify the issues.

Knowing how to relate to mentors can establish your future in a very real sense, for these relationships can help you participate with people of power and influence in real or near-real situations.

Don't forget, as you seek mentors, to be sure to find someone you can trust. There are lots of out-of-town "experts" going from one group to the next, but not all have the wisdom or experience to help you and your organization.

Also, when it comes to bringing in outside mentors within your organization, be sure to promote, promote, promote. Build credibility. Then, when the "hired gun" affirms what you've been trying to teach, the results can be extraordinary.

THE SEQUOIA

I have heard mentoring compared to the growth of California's giant evergreen trees known as sequoias. The analogy is worth repeating. The sequoia grows to be hundreds of feet tall and lives for more than a thousand years. Why does it grow to such proportions? For one thing, the tree feeds from its environment through its strong, wide-ranging roots.

But it does not just take from its environment; it also gives. By providing shelter and nutrition to neighboring plants and animals, the sequoia contributes 80% more to the forest environment than it takes. It drops its branches and needles to feed other life, enriching the environment in which it lives. When it dies, it "gives birth," and new evergreens grow in a ring from the mother tree.

HAL GOOCH ♦ *STREET SMARTS* ♦ Proverb 16 ♦ 10

Mentoring and motivational programs can do the same thing for you. As you receive benefits, you can grow and succeed. You also develop roots in your organization and begin to mentor other achievers, thus giving back more than you receive.

But there is something about sequoias and mentoring that carries equal importance. A sequoia never stops growing. As long as it lives, it maintains vital relationships with other trees, plants and animal life, developing and contributing to everything around it--simultaneously giving and receiving.

That is the true meaning of mentoring/coaching relationships. When mentors share their strengths with us, they are not only teaching us, but also are building and encouraging us. Likewise, we can affirm others by mentoring them. In so doing, we can further develop our own strengths. All of us have deep, inner strengths we can share with others. The ancient philosopher Marcus Aurelius said, "Within is the fountain of good, and it will forever bubble up if thou wilt ever dig."

Mentors are vital to our development as powerful people, and mentoring is vital to the maintenance of power. Both members of the coaching relationship win by increasing their power at no one else's expense. Much of what we learn in life is through personal experience. No small amount of our knowledge comes from our personal observation of others, which is the next best thing to getting personal experience. Through simple communication and subtle example, we learn from mentors. As a result, we develop power--or fail to develop it--by our choice of mentors, or role models.

Once learned, it is up to each of us to continue the mentoring circle of giving and receiving.

Proverb 17
"First impressions often make lasting impressions."

"We can all be geniuses because one definition of genius is the infinite capacity for taking pains. Perfection in details is essential. Generalities don't count!"

KNUTE ROCKNE
Legendary Notre Dame
"Fighting Irish" Football Coach

IMPRESSIONS

If there's any one thing that I enjoyed most about growing up in rural North Carolina, it was the way many Southerners spoke the language. We've lost some of that today, I'm afraid, in the world of malls and the Internet where fewer and fewer people simply get together to "jaw," as they called it. The closest thing to it today is to listen to a tape of my wonderful friend, the late country comedian Jerry Clower. Or read a book by the late humorist Lewis Grizzard. Just thinking about their tales makes me smile. Mostly I've loved the way they wove their molasses-and-honey stories around the phrases I remember from my childhood.

One saying, favored in the deep patrician South, and often ridiculed by Southern humorists, remains imbedded in my mind: "First impressions often make lasting impressions." I heard it lots of times during my youth but I didn't understand the true meaning until I went into business for myself. It was then that I saw that potential clients or colleagues don't take long to make up their minds. I remember making what I thought were great presentations, but before I got out of the proverbial "starting blocks," the person's eyes were already glancing at the clocks. Who knows what went wrong, but whatever happened took place within seconds of entering the person's office. It's a sobering lesson to learn how first impressions often make lasting impressions.

HAL GOOCH ♦ STREET SMARTS ♦ Proverb 17 ♦ 3

Through the years that well-worn phrase has been useful. It's helped me keep going, even when I didn't make good first impressions, knowing that I could get better. It's helped me seek to do whatever I could do to make better first impressions—reading books, listening to tapes, learning from good teachers and mentors. I learned to say "no" to self-doubts and negative influences and "yes" to positive ones.

And with time, I've become better at presenting myself, both with first impressions and lasting ones, by understanding how important it is to present myself as well as I can in every situation. Today, some call it "image." Others have labeled it "positioning." I simply call it making a good impression, and doing so can change your life. But making a good impression isn't just buying a new suit or shoes. It involves positioning yourself well in every area of your life.

Positioning

Positioning? Webster's New International Dictionary defines it as: ". . .a spot, situation or condition that conveys some advantage." Positioning means presenting yourself in the best light possible. It means, if you are a business owner, that you, your company and your products or services come to mind when your customers want to buy whatever your products or services may be.

Positioning is a combination of many elements: listening, dressing for success, planning, following through, marketplace knowledge, professional demeanor, integrity, goal-setting, time management, self-discipline and more. The secret is standing out from the crowd. Some call it differentiation. Others say it is definition. Mainly, it means that you are able to set your product, your company or organization and yourself apart from the crowd.

How do you "position" yourself better? Let me answer by giving you another saying: "You can't judge a book by its cover." It's a phrase that certainly holds true for most businesspeople. I've met many wonderful, competent, thoroughly professional men and women who appeared as if they'd slept in their clothes. And some famous people take delight at contravening what the public expects them to do, or wear, or say. But those exceptions just prove the rule. While some people are already known for their integrity, or savvy, or brilliance and they can flout this rule with delight, most better pay close attention to their image. A few patient souls in the general public are willing to look inside the book before judging, but most of the time what you are on the outside is what people see first. What they see and experience usually determines whether or not you will gain acceptance or inspire confidence with them.

If you want to achieve your goals, you must learn to position yourself for success. In other words, from the first impression, you must look the part you want to play.

THIRTY SECONDS

It has been said that when an actor auditions for a part, the director knows within 15 to 30 seconds whether he or she can use the actor, based on the actor's self-presentation. The same is true in life. Within 30 seconds of walking into a room where no one knows you, people will make several judgments about you, based on what how you look, talk and act.

Is it fair? Probably not. Is it true? Judge for yourself. People make snap decisions about other people. Why? As we mature, we develop filters to determine as much as possible as quickly as possible. What are those filters?

(1) Appearance

Good grooming and good health play a large role in how others perceive us. On the whole, people would rather deal with others who appear healthy and well-groomed rather than with persons who appear physically ill and disheveled. A good appearance suggests the presence of self-confidence. In turn, self-assurance tends to inspire others to return a growing measure of confidence.

(2) Clothing

Image consultants say that clothing really does make the man or woman. Up to 90% of our appearance depends on our choice of clothing. It can be vital to create a powerful image in the eyes of others. Granted, every business or social situation doesn't require a power suit, but you must be aware that your choices concerning clothing have a great deal to do with what others think about you, in terms of how you project credibility, confidence and competence.

(3) Posture

Some studies estimate that body language accounts for more than half of a first impression. Simple things such as posture influence the way others perceive and relate back to us. Yes, Mom really did have your best interests at heart when she nagged, "Stand up straight!"

The finest clothing you can buy won't overcome the negative image resulting from poor posture. The posture of a person who lacks confidence will reflect a lack of confidence. The posture of a self-confident person will reveal confidence.

(4) Handshake.

Your handshake is the quickest way to make or break a first impression. Limp, "dead fish" handshakes generally convey aloofness or weakness. A firm handshake conveys energy and interest.

One note of warning: Avoid handshakes that are too vigorous. There are few things more painful than a crushing grip, especially when you are wearing a ring. Men, especially, need to be careful of squeezing a woman's hand too hard.

(5) Eye contact

Too little eye contact indicates a lack of self-confidence; too much suggests arrogance and creates discomfort in the other party. Good eye contact is a sign of interest and self-confidence, provided it's administered in small doses. Don't stare, but don't look everywhere else.

(6) Voice

Your voice plays a significant role in first and lasting impressions. If it's too loud, it will irritate others. If it's too soft, others will tire of straining to hear you. Sloppy speech leaves people wondering what you said, but enunciating too carefully makes you sound phony. Talk too fast, and people wonder what you're selling, but talk too slowly and they'll become bored and impatient. If your tone is harsh, people will find you abrasive, but if you're too soft, people might not take you seriously. The same is true if your pitch is too high (childlike or nervous), or too low (artificial or trying to act older). An effective voice results from the right mix of the best qualities.

Tape yourself under a variety of situations. Use a tape recorder, as well, to seek to improve. If your voice isn't as warm or effective as you want it to be, seek the assistance of a good vocal coach. Take a public speaking course at local a college. Join Toastmasters. Whatever you do, learn to make the best of your voice. Think of the people who have affected you greatly throughout your life—teachers, ministers, actors, broadcasters. Chances are high that the person's voice was a huge part of the equation. A wonderful, powerful voice can convey the best image.

Image is vital to the way you position yourself in the marketplace. Granted, a successful image doesn't guarantee success. Success is a lifelong journey. However, image is a significant factor in the total impression a businessperson makes on the people around him or her.

SLIGHT EDGE

One of life's greatest secrets is quite simple: You don't have to be 100% smarter, better, faster or stronger than others to succeed. Not even 50% or 20%. In almost every field of endeavor, you can be a phenomenal success by building only a marginal advantage over others. What do I mean?

You have heard of "winning by a nose." It happens all the time. Many Olympic medals have been won by hundredths of seconds. World championships have been decided by one hit, one touchdown or one swish of the net. Races, including the Kentucky Derby, NASCAR and NHRA, have been determined by inches. The greatest golf tournaments have come down to one final putt during a sudden-death ending.

"Winning by a nose," or the marginal advantage phenomenon occurs outside sports, as well. In 1960, John F. Kennedy defeated Richard M. Nixon by only 113,000 votes, one-half vote per precinct. Political analysts since then point to the crucial television debate when JFK's tousled hair and warmth edged Nixon's five o'clock shadow and cold demeanor. Kennedy's people had simply done a slightly better job of preparation.

HAL GOOCH ♦ *STREET SMARTS* ♦ Proverb 17 ♦ 9

Here's the point: Attention to detail—that slight-edge advantage—can make all the difference in the world to you as a businessperson. Marginal advantage is the center fielder's extra-fast step to the left. It is a business manager's last check of an important proposal. It may even be Godiva chocolates on the pillows of a turned-down bed as a hotel chain strives to provide one more reason for you to keep coming back.

What does this mean for you? Whether you are a CEO, business owner, salesperson, middle manager or frontline worker, your professional success will undoubtedly depend on being a percent or two better than others are. But here's the proverbial "catch:" The marginal advantage doesn't come easy. It requires extra effort. But those small, supposedly insignificant differences between you and your competitors can mean everything.

Remember, the secret of success for every successful person lies in the fact that he or she has developed a habit of doing things that others don't like to do. Positioning yourself better calls for a whole new way of thinking and acting. You can join that select group of high achievers by becoming a master at image, preparation and confidence. Confidence comes when you make a great impression. Then image and positioning help your influence in the marketplace. If you can influence others positively, you can help them achieve their goals. When you help enough people attain their dreams, you then reach your own. It can be a wonderful cycle when fueled by the win-win philosophy, and it all begins by making a good first impression. Based on that first impression, you can propel lasting success by positioning yourself positively!

Proverb 18
"Don't reinvent the wheel."

*"If I have seen further it is by
standing upon the shoulders of giants."*
Sir Isaac Newton

HAL GOOCH ♦ STREET SMARTS ♦ Proverb 18 ♦ 2

NOTHING NEW UNDER THE SUN

There's no need to reinvent the wheel. In fact, there are few things in life that are truly original. You'll notice that I took my own advice when I wrote this book—nothing is completely new and revolutionary. Most of these Proverbs, in fact, have been gleaned from some of the best lessons I've learned over the past five decades. Human nature, after all, hasn't changed much in the past few thousand years.

Here's the point: Most great achievements in life come on top of the foundations built by others. History, in fact, is filled with examples of inventions and advancements that were made by people who used the advancements and knowledge of others to bring about breakthroughs:

☐ Christopher Columbus did not discover the New World. The Asiatic peoples who became Native Americans were certainly the first. Norse expeditions to North America, starting with Bjarni Herjolfsson in 986, are established historically. Leif Erickson had settlements on the North American coast 500 years before Queen Isabella financed the voyage of the *Nina*, *Pinta* and *Santa Maria*. However, Columbus forever destroyed the "flat earth" myth enroute to initiating widespread two-way commerce between the Old and New Worlds. Previous discoveries were so little known that even the best-educated Europeans were unaware of the existence of America prior to Columbus. The "Admiral of the Ocean Sea," unlike any of his predecessors, forever changed the concept of our world

- During 1820, the Danish physicist Hans Christian Oersted, at the end of a lecture, happened to put a wire conducting an electric current near a magnet. That "accident" laid the foundation for additional research that showed when a current passes through a wire, it acts as if it were a magnet. To understand what Oersted had discovered, Michael Faraday repeated his experiments, varying conditions to explore the phenomenon. In the course of this research, he discovered that current through a wire could make a magnetic needle circle around it. In order confirm and demonstrate this discovery, Faraday invented the first electromagnetic motor.

- Henry Ford did not invent the automobile, of course, but he was the first to develop mass production; as a result, his Model Ts revolutionized his generation and gave almost everyone the opportunity to join the automobile age.

- During the 1940s, Percy Spencer and several of his fellow scientists at Raytheon used a radar instrument to cook popcorn and eggs. No one really had an idea what to do with the new technology, so it was 1955 before Tappan built the concept into a home microwave oven, but it did not become a practical, affordable possibility until Amana began making the Radarange in 1967. This curious oddity has since changed the cooking and eating habits of America. Can you imagine life without the ability to instantly "nuke" popcorn, pizza and pie?

HAL GOOCH ♦ *STREET SMARTS* ♦ Proverb 18 ♦ 4

☐ Walt Disney did not come up with the idea of an amusement park. In fact, the amusement park concept is actually tied back to Medieval Pleasure Palaces. In America, buoyed by the success of the 1893 World's Fair in Chicago (where the Ferris Wheel was unveiled), eventually 1,500 amusement parks were in operation throughout the United States previous to the Crash of 1929, the Great Depression and World War Two. Significant were New York's Coney Island, Atlantic City's Steel Pier, Ohio's Cedar Point and Myrtle Beach's Palladium.

Then came a new concept from the whimsical mind of the creator of Mickey Mouse. When Disneyland first opened in 1955, many people were skeptical that an amusement park without any of the traditional attractions would succeed. But Disneyland was different. Instead of a midway, Disneyland offered five distinct theme areas, providing "guests" with the fantasy of travel to different lands and times. With 3.8 million visitors the first year, Disneyland was an immediate success, and as a result, the theme park era was born.

☐ In the 1960s and 1970s, 3M chemist Spencer Silver knew there was something special about his tacky adhesive. He shopped his little vials of glue around the company for five years. The substance was refined by Henry Courtney and Roger Merrill and nurtured to by Arthur Fry, who first used the little slips of paper to mark places in his hymnal while singing at his church. The Post-it Note was born, and Silver's "failed" adhesive became the key ingredient of what today is 3M's best-selling product.

HAL GOOCH ♦ *STREET SMARTS* ♦ Proverb 18 ♦ 5

☐ The Walkman, brought to life during 1978 by Mitsuro Ida and a group of Sony's electronics engineers in Tokyo, was another accidental product that was built on the foundation of numerous developments. Originally designed to record and playback stereophonic sounds, it was deemed too large with the complex speakers attached. Then someone at Sony decided to remove the speakers and add one simple modification to the design—lightweight stereo speakers. Suddenly the machine became the best-selling electronic device in the world during the late Seventies and early Eighties. What would the past generation have done without their Walkman and Walkman wannabes?

Very often, when people say, "It can't be done," they are actually wondering if anything good can come from all the information they have in front of them. Success is often in the execution. HOW you do something is often more important than WHAT you decide to do. Remember, Walt Disney didn't invent amusement parks, Henry Ford didn't invent the car, Bill Gates didn't invent software and Christopher Columbus didn't discover America but they all changed the world building on something already there.

STRATEGIES

So how do you build great achievements on the foundations of others? How do you avoid "reinventing the wheel?" Here are several key guidelines:

HAL GOOCH ♦ *STREET SMARTS* ♦ Proverb 18 ♦ 6

(1) **Give credit.**

Whatever you do in life, you will be building your success on the successes of others. Acknowledge them. Honor them. Empower them. It's amazing how greatness grows as the credit spreads.

(2) **Count your costs.**

Commitment to your goals does not come cheaply. The bigger the dream, the more expensive it is. However, once you have counted costs and made a definite commitment, you should be able to develop a solid strategy plan. Count your costs by seeking advice and counseling from others who have gone before you.

There is always an element of risk. In fact, if you take the risk out of life, you take out the opportunity. When you play baseball, you cannot get from one base to the next unless you are willing to give up the security of standing securely on the square bag. You must also embrace a certain level of risk in order to reach new dreams on any level. The secret is calculating and controlling the amount of risk as you take the next step, and you can do that best by gauging your risk by others who have blazed trails before you.

(3) **Build a network of family, friends and associates with whom you can share your dreams.**

Developing dreams with others means more than you can imagine. Getting people to work with you is more than a quick-fix--it must be bought with the price of opening yourself to others, trusting them to do a good job, encouraging their growth, and giving them positive reinforcement on a job well done.

If you have not built a network of friends and co-workers--people who rely on you, with whom you can trust vital information and to whom you can turn in times of crisis--you are missing a key ingredient in the strategy of building on the foundations of others.

In business, on an athletic field, in politics and at home, you need a lot of people, spread out in the right places, on whom you can depend (and vice versa). A network is not something that can be established overnight. Your network will require nurturing, but you must develop a strong, supportive group of co-workers and friends.

Just remember: A network is a mutually helpful, flexible group of associates and friends. You cannot build that structure easily. You must be willing to give much more than you get. By giving unselfishly--giving more than you get--you receive much more than you realize. Good things come back to you and become a vital part of your success.

HAL GOOCH ♦ *STREET SMARTS* ♦ Proverb 18 ♦ 8

You have so many things going for you when you seek to accomplish something worthwhile, especially when you relax and give up the effort of reinventing the wheel. The Law of Reciprocity--what we sow we will reap--only works when you are sowing "seeds" and cultivating "ground" unselfishly. You can also experience the Serendipity Effect--being in the right place at the right time and somehow the team and vital resources come unexpectedly.

New insights or advancements seldom involve new information. They almost always the result of a new way of looking at what you already know. Many times, in fact, finding enough resources involves knowing what to do with the information and assets that are even now available to you. Time after time, in business and consulting, I have found that as you step out to reach for your dreams, the resources become available.

More importantly, very few things in life require all of the resources in advance. You must count the costs realistically, of course, but that doesn't mean that you can never do anything until all the resources are in hand.

RECOGNITION

When you build your successes on the foundation of others, your learn to recognize so many assets which are available. You have courage, intuition, unseen laws of nature and unrealized talents. You have people waiting to help you. You have a

HAL GOOCH ♦ *STREET SMARTS* ♦ Proverb 18 ♦ 9

wealth of inner reserves to help insure success every step of the way. The secret is learning to tap into those often-hidden treasures.

Resources may mean money, knowledge, contacts in the right places, skills, more people--whatever it takes to achieve your dreams. The bigger your dreams, the greater your need for resources.

Avoid reinventing the wheel. Success means building on the foundations that others have built. The greatest gift in life is not things, but the ability to use your experience and the wisdom of others to make the most of your opportunities!

Proverb 19
"Keep your eyes on the clock."

"If time be of all things most precious, wasting time must be the greatest prodigality, since lost time is never found again; and what we call time enough always proves little enough. Let us then be up and doing, and doing to a purpose; so by diligence shall we do more with less perplexity."

**Benjamin Franklin
Inventor, Printer,
Statesman and Author**

VALUABLE RESOURCE

Thousands of time-management books have been written during the past hundred years. Let me condense all of them down to one sentence: *Time-management is actually self-management.*

But before you can become a successful time- or self-manager, you need to ask yourself these three questions:

- ☐ What are my time-habits?
- ☐ What are my time-wasters?
- ☐ How can I become a better manager of my time?

Let's take those questions one at a time.

TIME-HABITS

The most pressing question about activities is not, "What are you doing?" but rather, "Why are you doing it?" Wasting motion is wasting time; and wasting time is wasting your life. You must learn to focus on your top priorities and not get swamped by a rising whirlpool of activities.

The first step in managing your life is knowing precisely where you spend your hours. How do you spend your time working? Playing? Planning?

Here is a very effective tactic for analyzing your time habits: Keep a time log. Keep a record of each 30-minute block for a week. Undoubtedly, you will discover patterns that you may want to change. I have done this many times in life and have sometimes been shocked at time-wasters.

You will probably find that there are different times of the day and week in which you tend to waste more time than others. This information will give you a basis for improving your schedule. You will also discover that you are more productive at certain times of the day. Bolstered by this information, you can sometimes schedule important tasks during your best times.

After you have kept a detailed log for a week, analyze the specific activities that get the largest amounts of time and rate them by importance. There must be some reason why successful people, almost without exception, keep periodic, specific time logs. You can profit from their example.

TIME-WASTERS

Once you determine time patterns, you can begin identifying and eliminating wasteful habits which rob you of your most vital possession—your life! Here are the most common ways to waste time:

(1) Failure to set time-priorities

(2) Poor, ineffective or misuse of time-management technology (telephone, voicemail, email, faxes)

(3) Procrastination

(4) Busywork

(5) Unnecessary or too-long meetings

(6) Failure to delegate tasks to capable people

(7) Shuffling the same paperwork again and again

(8) Poorly designed systems, red-tape or obsolete procedures

Which time-wasters can you add to the list? Once you have identified them, work on eliminating anything that chips away at this most-valuable resource. You have everything to gain.

STREET SMARTS TIME-MANAGEMENT

Reducing and even eliminating poor time habits may be one of the toughest challenges you will ever face. How can you begin to forge better time- and self-management patterns? Let me share the best that I have found:

(1) Focus on the benefits of better time-management.

Seldom do you do anything for no reason. Find your incentive and you reach your goals more quickly. Eliminating procrastination and time-misuse is a huge positive step toward a life with less stress, more quality free-time, more enjoyment, higher self-esteem and more money. Imagine yourself totally in control of your time. How would your life change?

(2) **Start now, not later.**

There are always plenty of reasons to wait until a better day to get organized. Get started now. Don't try to change everything at once. Start small, then keep making gradual improvement. After all, the easiest way to break a bad habit is to start a new, good habit. The least productive people in the world are not necessarily lazy; they're just disorganized. Don't just shuffle papers, process them. In fact, whenever possible, never pick up a sheet of paper more than once. Keep your life uncluttered by making good choices.

(3) **Set up victories for yourself.**

Create an inventory of tasks and projects that have been hanging around for a long time, then set up a realistic schedule for getting them done. Make the process a mental game, then reward yourself.

(4) **Tackle unpleasant tasks as early as possible each day.**

The later you schedule difficult projects, the easier it is to put them off until the next day. If your hate writing reports, do them first. If you dislike making contact or prospecting calls, handle them as soon as possible or they will handle you.

(5)   **Use visual reminders.**

"Do it now!" and "Time is money!" are both good starter signs. Many entrepreneurial, corporate, academic and athletic champions use positive reminders; why not follow their examples? Granted, slogans are mere words unless you follow-through, but I've noticed that the highest achievers, with few exceptions, surround themselves with inspirational sayings, Bible verses and mottoes for living.

(6)   **Concentrate on results, not activities.**

Generally, people get 80% of their results from 20% of their activities. Do the math for your own life. Now, what if you would consciously devote more than 20% of your time focused on your most profitable and beneficial activities?

Think RESULTS, not busywork! Learn how to weed out more and more of your least-productive activities.

(7)   **Learn to delegate.**

Learn **what** to delegate. Learn **how** to delegate. Learn **to whom** you can delegate. This will mean that you can no longer do everything, but you may be surprised at your increased effectiveness when you learn how to empower others.

(8) Manage interruptions.

Protect your most productive times by avoiding the urgent-but-unimportant interference's. The telephone never seems to stop ringing, doesn't it, when you've got to finish important paperwork? The best television program always seem to be scheduled during times when you need to think through that major business plan, don't they? You will either manage interruptions or they will control your days.

(9) Become a championship planner.

The master key to all effective time-management is planning. Keep priorities straight with "to do" lists. "To-do lists are one of most practical lessons I've ever learned," Charles Schwab, the late founder of Bethlehem Steel, is reported to have said. "I had put off making a phone call for nine months, so I decided to list it as my number one task on the next day's agenda. That call netted us two million dollars because of a new order for steel beams." From that moment Schwab is said to have became an avid fan of "to do" lists.

Planning is one of the best ways to ensure that you concentrate on important goals and tasks. By the way, many believe that the best time to write out your "to do" list is at night. You symbolically unclutter your mind as you write, and you start the day already in gear. What could be better?

(10) Work hard, then play hard.

Enjoy your free time. Nowhere is self-discipline more important than in the matter of taking time to recharge your batteries and smell the roses. For some people, this means planning family weekends and vacations. For others, reaching goals involves participation in hobbies or events. Going without any kind of free time is counterproductive. Otherwise, you always be operating with your batteries low and produce below your capacity. Work hard, of course, but play hard, too!

FOCUS AND FIND

Anytime you are faced with the fact that you aren't producing all that you are capable of doing, you have to look deeply into your heart for the reasons. Once you realize that you are not using your time wisely, for example, you have two choices:

- ☐ Change the situation.
- ☐ Change yourself.

The happiest people in life seem to be the ones who can face life honestly, making whatever changes they need to make and focusing on their highest priorities!

How about you? Instead of having a life filled with stress and unrealistic workloads, how would you like to be successful and fulfilled more of the time? Start by

HAL GOOCH ♦ *STREET SMARTS* ♦ **Proverb 19 ♦ 9**

placing greater value on your time. Refuse to allow time to hold you hostage. Only you know how much you can do if you eliminate your time-wasters and learn to control your environment.

Organize your life and produce extraordinary results!

Proverb 20
"Persistence pays."

"Nothing in the world can take the place of persistence. Talent will not; nothing is more common than unsuccessful men with talent. Genius will not; unrewarded genius is almost a proverb. Education will not; the world is full of educated derelicts. Persistence and determination alone are omnipotent."

CALVIN COOLIDGE
U.S. President

HAL GOOCH ♦ *STREET SMARTS* ♦ Proverb 20 ♦ 2

IRON MAN

I love watching the Summer Olympic Games every four years. I don't follow most of the sports during the other years—fishing is my preference—but there's something about the Olympics that touches emotions deeply. If I asked you to tell me your favorite Olympic memory, you would probably have trouble narrowing down the choices. It's that way around the world.

Though I wasn't alive when Glenn Cunningham ran the mile in the Olympics, I am still touched by reading his story that took a dramatic turn during back in the Winter of 1916. It was a cold, blustery morning. As usual, the four Cunningham children arrived early at the small wooden schoolhouse near Elkhart, Kansas. While their sister stayed outdoors to play on the swing, seven-year-old Glenn and an older brother played tic-tac-toe on the blackboard while Floyd, the oldest boy, began building a fire in the potbellied stove. Floyd poured what he thought was kerosene into the stove. The boy didn't know that the school had been used the previous evening for a meeting by a community organization. Gasoline, not kerosene, was in the can, and the coals at the bottom of the stove were still red-hot.

Instantly, a massive explosion rocked the schoolhouse! The wooden structure became a blazing inferno. Glenn attempted to climb on top of a desk to get his feet and legs out of the flames, but his clothes were already on fire. Somehow the three boys made it outside. Their sister threw dirt and sand on them to smother the flames. In a state of shock, the Cunningham children helped each other run the two miles back home. When they arrived, a doctor was summoned, but he was 11 miles away and would take hours to arrive. All three boys sustained massive injuries. Nine days later, Floyd died.

Glenn's legs were severely burned. For several days, the doctor pondered whether or not to amputate the young boy's charred legs. Glenn's parents were told that even if he lived, which was still doubtful, he would never walk again.

After many weeks, the doctor was able to tell Glenn to get up. He meant that Glenn could begin sitting up in bed and looking out the window. Glenn thought the doctor meant that he could get up and go outside to play. He swung himself out of bed and attempted to stand. But he had no feeling or strength in his legs, and he collapsed in a heap beside the bed.

The doctor then sadly told Glenn, "I'm sorry son, but you will never walk again."

"I will walk. I know I will," Glenn cried as they put him back into bed.

Not only did Glenn eventually walk, forcing his legs to stretch and move, but in time he started running. He won his first race as a fourth grader running against high school boys. He ran his way through collegiate and AAU (American Athletic Union) events, setting the record for the world's fastest mile in 1934.

During the 1930s, the "Iron Man of Kansas," burned up the tracks, especially as he became a favorite on the Saturday night radio broadcasts of track and field events from Madison Square Garden. He represented America in two Olympics, winning the silver medal in 1932. In the 1980s, he was voted the greatest track and field performer in the history of Madison Square Garden.

In keeping with his strong belief in persistence, he received a bachelor's degree from Kansas University, a master's in education from the University of Iowa and his doctorate from New York University. Not only did he become a popular college professor, but he and his beloved wife Ruth established the Christian Youth Ranch in Arkansas and gave a helping hand and a home to hundreds of troubled youth.

Glenn passed away several years ago, but one thing he said has stuck with me:

"A person must face every situation honestly. The Lord never made a failure, but we often make failures of ourselves. We can change that. We can just pass each test, as it faces us. If we set goals and never give up, we can achieve whatever we set out to do."

To anyone who saw him run on those scarred legs or who saw him working with young people, Glenn Cunningham was living proof that anyone who is persistent enough can do almost anything—in athletics, in life, at home, in business.

PERSISTENCE

In every man and woman's life, there are times of summit-like challenges--either through defeats or failures. Relatively few people use such tests as opportunities to become stronger, better-equipped performance managers. The majority, by far, allow these ordeals of life to annihilate their dreams.

Persistence is a great difference-maker. It is one of the most effective keys you can use to overcome every challenge you face. That's why I've waited until the final Proverb in STREET SMARTS to talk about persistence. You see, life does not always grant your first dream, or your second or even your hundredth. Along with your triumphs and successes, you will face setbacks, heartbreaks, tragedies and unavoidable problems.

HAL GOOCH ♦ *STREET SMARTS* ♦ Proverb 20 ♦ 5

While most people tend to lose heart and surrender their dreams during life's horrible times, you can learn these strategies for re-igniting your dreams.

(1) Persistence will help you understand the difference between temporary setbacks and permanent losses.

You learned in seventh grade science, "For every action, there is an equal and opposite reaction." If you do anything in life, anything at all, you will encounter opposition. It is a fact. Still, you cannot turn back every time you run into a wall. It's not always easy to tell the difference between a stepping stone and a stumbling block, especially when the object seems to be ten feet tall.

Nobody, but nobody, wins every skirmish or goes through life unscathed. If you cannot conquer every foe, the secret is to decide which victories are worth fighting for, and which are not.

(2) Persistence teaches you that obstacles are there to strengthen you.

Everyone faces challenges. Life is often unfair. Your dreams, if they are vital to you, will be tested. Some people see these problems as gigantic reasons for quitting. Others, for whatever reason, see challenges as a reason to get stronger, to become better and to seek more wisdom. Weightlifting, for crying out loud, is a barrier, but athletes use these weights to help them become stronger and achieve greater goals.

HAL GOOCH ♦ *STREET SMARTS* ♦ Proverb 20 ♦ 6

(3) Persistence shows you one of the main reasons for obstacles—to give higher and higher standards to measure your growing strength.

How do you know how far you've come if you never face any opposition? Olympic runners, for example, seldom balk at the idea of preliminary heats, for they know they can see where they stand, by comparison, against the other runners. What tennis or golfer would consider it unreasonable to work up through the amateur and professional ranks? Whatever you face as a fledgling businessperson is a stepping stone AND a measuring stick.

You show maturity, in any area of life, when you understand persistence, for you learn to view each challenge as another chance to get stronger. If you quit, at any level, you lose momentum and nerve.

BEYOND DEFEAT

As difficult as it may seem, all problems can make you stronger. Many years ago I saw the words to this verse written by an unknown poet. It's been handed around for years, continues to bounce around on the internet and remains an inspiration to me:

Cripple him, and you have a Sir Walter Scott.
Lock him in a prison cell, and you have a John Bunyan.
Bury him in the snows of Valley Forge, and you have a George Washington.
Raise him in abject poverty, and you have an Abraham Lincoln.
Subject him to bitter religious prejudice, and you have a Disraeli.

HAL GOOCH ♦ *STREET SMARTS* ♦ Proverb 20 ♦ 7

Afflict him with asthma as a child, and you have a Theodore Roosevelt.

Stab him with rheumatic pains until he can't sleep without an opiate, and you have a Steinmetz.

Put him in a grease pit of a locomotive roundhouse, and you have a Walter P. Chrysler.

Make him play second fiddle in an obscure South American orchestra, and you have a Toscanini.

At birth, deny her the ability to see, hear, and speak, and you have a Helen Keller.

May I add a line about one of my heroes: *Burn and disfigure his legs as a child, and you have the world-famous Olympic miler, Glenn Cunningham.*

Difficulties actually accelerate your development, especially when you understand the value of barriers. Muscles never got stronger from ease. Courage and character never developed in an inactive, boring life.

Sooner or later, you will be forced to answer the question: "How much will it take to stop you?" It's a question that only you can answer.

Success and barriers are almost always linked. I don't know anyone who has achieved very much without suffering from bad judgement, defeats and failures—yet came back stronger than before. Be glad for your setbacks. Problems and failures are great starting points for your lifelong pursuit of success.

HAL GOOCH ♦ *STREET SMARTS* ♦ Proverb 20 ♦ 8

Persistence is the key, and persistence simply means refusing to give up while getting wiser, stronger and more motivated to succeed--no matter what happens!

A Final Word

"Too often we act as if the future is something that happens to us, rather than something each of us creates every single day. Many people spend more time talking about where they have been than where they are or where they are going. Here's the truth: The past is over—it is unchangeable. So invest your time in today and tomorrow."

FOCUS

The Argonne National Laboratory, near Chicago, is one of America's major atomic research and development establishments. This laboratory can trace its history to the beginning of organized nuclear research in the United States. Here, a staff of 1200 scientists and engineers devote themselves to scientific research.

One of the most remarkable sights in the laboratory is a simple glass case in a basement room. The case stands next to an electronic computer and bears the inscription: "In case of emergency, break glass." Inside the shiny case is a simple abacus, like those used in Oriental lands for centuries. The abacus is there to keep the cutting-edge scientists humble as a stark reminder that the most precise and expensive scientific instruments cannot cope or measure everything in life.

It's a lesson everyone should learn, especially STREET SMART businesspeople.

SUCCESS AND FAILURE

Life is often unpredictable. What worked yesterday may not work today. Therefore, it is vital that you learn to handle life's ups-and-downs. Having a realistic understanding of both sides of life's coin will help you sustain greater success down the road!

Success and power can corrupt. So can failure and disillusionment. The secret is learning how to handle not only the extremes of life, but also what happens between the peaks. Therefore, I'd like to leave you with four simple guidelines that are condensed from the pages of STREET SMARTS:

(1) **Define, sooner rather than later, what success means to you.**

A clear definition will help you keep eventual success in perspective. Fantasyland is a fun place to visit at Disney World, but you cannot live there. Likewise, you cannot allow yourself to live in an unrealistic dream world.

Too many people pin their hopes for success on winning a bundle at Vegas or Atlantic City. Or we dream of winning a $50 million lottery. Statistically, you have a better chance of getting hit by lightning—twice! Gambling showplaces and lotteries are designed to get as much of your money as possible, while giving away only enough to get you to try again. Some things never change.

Success is a journey, not a destination. Achieving success does not mean that you leave reality, failure, or problems behind. There are few quick-fixes out there and those who have achieved prominence with "get-rich-quick" schemes statistically self-implode. Anything worthwhile takes time, energy and a fierce determination—plus lots of faith.

(2) **Focus on today and tomorrow, not your past.**

Why have I reminded you in Proverb after Proverb, to become a powerful dreamer and goal-setter? It's because every true success I've met is a champion at setting realistic and worthwhile short, mid, and long-range goals.

Your own options are as bright as you want them to be. Tomorrow's crucial need is for more people than ever to understand STREET SMARTS principles. You can take charge of your life by understanding and preparing yourself today for tomorrow's great achievements.

Best of all, no matter what happens, tomorrow is a new day! That fact, in itself, is one of the most important lessons you will learn in life.

(3) **Treat failure and success as the same.**

Every life has both victories and losses. Stand apart from both and examine why each occurred to you. You show your true character in situations at either end of the spectrum. Frankly, that is what true freedom is--doing your best and accepting the results.

(4) **Spend time with people who love you for YOU, not for your successes.**

Being with people who care for you for the right reasons helps place your feet squarely on the ground and keeps your head out of the clouds. Honor your family. Build a network of friends and colleagues. The relationships you build will help you face life's most oppressive challenges.

There you have it—everything condensed down to four points. If we can learn these lessons well and use them wisely, we can look forward to a lifetime of success! I challenge you! Recognize and grasp your God-given talents. Use these timeless principles that have brought success and fulfillment to so many businesspersons who have blazed the trail before you.

Write down what kind of person you want to be. Invest time to become that person. Choose your roads carefully. Travel with patience. And you will discover how wonderful the journey can be. You will turn your dreams into reality and touch the lives of thousands of others. It doesn't take a genius. It just takes a little *STREET SMARTS*, one day at a time!"